13 most important BIBLE Lessons

for kids about living for JESUS

D1283681

Group

Loveland, Colorado
group.com

Group resources really work!

This Group resource incorporates our R.E.A.L. approach to ministry. It reinforces a growing friendship with Jesus, encourages long-term learning, and results in life transformation, because it's

Relational
Learner-to-learner interaction enhances learning and builds Christian friendships.

Experiential
What learners experience through discussion and action sticks with them up to 9 times longer than what they simply hear or read.

Applicable
The aim of Christian education is to equip learners to be both hearers and doers of God's Word.

Learner-based
Learners understand and retain more when the learning process takes into consideration how they learn best.

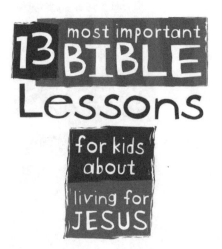

Copyright © 2014 Group Publishing, Inc

All rights reserved. No part of this book may be reproduced in any manner whatsoever without prior written permission from the publisher, except where noted in the text and in the case of brief quotations embodied in critical articles and reviews. For information, visit group.com/permissions.

Visit our website: group.com

CREDITS
Contributing Authors: Jody Brolsma, Mikal Keefer, Amy Nappa, Siv M. Ricketts, Amy Weaver, Jill Wuellner
Editors: Jennifer Hooks, Lee Sparks, Christine Yount Jones
Assistant Editor: Becky Helzer
Cover Design: Rebecca Swain
Book Design: Jean Bruns
Production: Suzi Jensen and Kate Elvin

Unless otherwise indicated, all Scripture quotations are taken from the *Holy Bible* New Living Translation, copyright © 1996, 2004, 2007. Used by permission of Tyndale House Publishers, Inc. Carol Stream, Illinois 60188. All rights reserved.

ISBN 978-1-4707-0427-8

10 9 8 7 6 5 4 3 2   19 18 17 16 15

Printed in the United States of America.

CONTENTS

INTRODUCTION

Ask people who minister to children what they want most, and you'll hear something like this:

"I want kids to know the Bible."

"I want children to have a strong relationship with God."

"I want kids to have a faith foundation that'll stand the test of time."

That's what the *13 Most Important Bible Lessons for Kids* series is all about—helping kids build a strong foundation in the basics of their faith. In *13 Most Important Bible Lessons for Kids About Living for Jesus,* you'll draw children closer to Jesus and help them learn through his example and those who followed him how to live for our Savior. Based on the prayer that Jesus offered for his disciples in John 17, each lesson uses Scripture, conversation, and hands-on experiences to teach kids vital truths that include:

Jesus' followers obey God's Word. (John 17:6)

Jesus' followers accept God's gifts through faith. (John 17:7-8)

Jesus' followers belong to God. (John 17:9)

Jesus' followers bring glory to Jesus. (John 17:10, 14)

Jesus' followers live in the world but aren't of it. (John 17:11)

Jesus' followers trust in God's protection. (John 17:12)

Jesus' followers are filled with joy. (John 17:13)

Jesus' followers are made holy by God's truth. (John 17:17, 19)

Jesus' followers are sent into mission. (John 17:18)

Jesus' followers share their faith with others. (John 17:20)

Jesus' followers unite with each other. (John 17:21, 23)

Jesus' followers look forward to heaven. (John 17:24)

Jesus' followers stay close to Jesus. (John 17:25-26).

These lessons won't fill your kids with theoretical information they'll soon forget. Instead, we've designed the lessons to transform your kids by engaging them in learning experiences that'll help them know the loving God who created them and sustains them.

7

Here's the flow for each lesson:

Set the Foundation—Engages kids in an opening activity to get them enthused and wanting more.

Present the Bible Foundation—This is the "meat" of the lesson, designed to help kids dig into the Bible.

Build on the Foundation—Once kids have learned a key attribute of God, they respond and apply what they've learned in a meaningful way—then pray.

Jesus told a much-loved parable about the need to build a strong faith foundation. You know the parable: The wise man built his house upon the rock…and nothing could tear down that house!

This is what you dream of, plan for, and pray about in ministry—that the children you minister to will have such a strong faith foundation that nothing will be able to tear down their faith. May God use *13 Most Important Bible Lessons for Kids About Living for Jesus* as you lead children in their growing relationship with Jesus.

Be aware that some children have food allergies that can be dangerous. Know your children, and consult with parents about allergies their children may have. Also be sure to read food labels carefully as hidden ingredients can cause allergy-related problems.

To avoid choking hazards, be sure to pick up pieces of any broken balloons promptly. Balloons may contain latex.

LESSON 1

Jesus' Followers Obey God's Word

The concept of obedience tends to be easy for kids to understand—it's the basis of much of what they learn at a young age. Obedience, though, can be a difficult concept to consistently apply. Kids may know what they *should* do—and what parents, teachers, or even the Bible says is *right* to do—but willfulness and selfishness arise and they tend to choose a different path.

How do we obey? By making a choice. And even when that choice is difficult, Jesus is here to guide us. The Bible lights our path. And other Christians can shore us up with encouragement and affirmation. As you lead kids in this lesson, let them know that the Bible is our go-to guide for direction in life—and that you and other Christian friends will be here to cheer kids on as they seek to obey and follow Jesus.

Scripture Foundation

LUKE 5:1-11

Simon obeys when Jesus tells him to toss the fishing nets again.

JOHN 14:15

Jesus says those who love him keep his commandments.

JAMES 1:22-25

We don't just read or listen to God's Word—we also obey it.

9

THIS LESSON AT A GLANCE

SEQUENCE	EXPERIENCES	SUPPLIES
SET THE FOUNDATION (about 10 minutes)	**Do It Like This** Kids play a game to see whether they can obey directions.	• none
PRESENT THE BIBLE FOUNDATION (about 25 minutes)	**Fishing Frenzy** Kids act out portions of Luke 5:1-11 to consider what it meant for Simon to obey Jesus.	• 5-foot lengths of yarn or string (1 per child) • scissors • 2 adult helpers for every 10 kids
BUILD ON THE FOUNDATION (about 10 minutes)	**Mirror, Mirror** Kids make a reminder to place on their mirrors, helping them look for ways to obey God's Word.	• kid-friendly Bible (preferably NLT) • mirror • 6-inch length of yarn or string • scissors • fine-tipped markers • large sticky notes (2 per person)

Do It Like This

(about 10 minutes)

Welcome children, and invite them to stand so they can all see you. You may choose to stand in a circle or have children scattered about the room.

SAY:

Let's play a game where you try to do whatever I do. Here's the tricky part: I'll say one thing and I might do that same thing, but I might do something different from what I say. You have to do what I do, no matter what I say.

For example, I'll say, "Jump on one foot. Do it like this." And then I might not jump on one foot, but I might do a jumping jack instead. You must do what I do, no matter what I say. Ready?

Spin in a circle. Do it like this. (Spin in a circle.)

Pat your head. Do it like this. (Jump up and down.)

Clap your hands. Do it like this. (Scratch your nose.)

Continue playing, alternating between doing and saying the same motion and doing and saying different motions. Invite children to take turns being the leader to see if they can confuse each other with saying one thing and doing something different.

When everyone has run out of ideas for funny ways to "do it like this," have children sit in a circle.

ASK:

• **What made it easy or difficult to obey the leader in our game?**

• **When have you had a person tell you to do one thing with their words, but then do something different through their actions?**

• **What makes it easy or difficult for you to obey your parents or teachers?**

SAY:

In a game, it's fun to try following and obeying. But sometimes there are people who tell us to do one thing, but then they do something

11

different. For instance, if you hear a doctor say "Don't smoke" but later you see that doctor in the parking lot smoking a cigarette, that can be confusing.

God's Word, the Bible, doesn't try to confuse us or trick us. The Bible gives us clear directions about what's right and wrong. When we're followers of Jesus, we obey God's Word. Today we're going to discover more about what it means to obey God's Word. Let's dig into that now.

PRESENT THE BIBLE FOUNDATION

Fishing Frenzy

(about 25 minutes)

Have kids sit in a circle, far enough apart that only their fingertips can touch. (If you have a group of more than 10, form two circles. You'll need two helpers for each circle.)

SAY:

Let's look at an example in the Bible of a person who obeyed even when the directions seemed strange. Give each child a 5-foot length of yarn.

Now, let's imagine what happened. Have kids lie down in place on the floor on their backs, feet facing into the circle, and close their eyes.

Picture in your mind what I tell you based on Luke 5:1-11. No matter what I tell you to do, you must keep your eyes closed until I tell you to open them. Your yarn is your net, so hold an end in each hand. Ready? Cast your net above your head. Have kids release one end of their net and let it stay there.

Simon was a fisherman. Simon would go out in a boat, throw his huge net into the water, and wait. And wait. And wait. Remain silent for 30 long seconds. During this time, have your helpers discreetly gather the ends of all the yarn and hold onto them.

12

SAY:

When Simon pulled in his net, sometimes there were lots of fish. Have kids gently tug on their "nets" while you or a helper holds the ends to show the resistance a lot of fish would give. **Sometimes there were none.** Let go of the nets and have kids tug on their nets again. **No fish meant Simon and his family would go hungry.**

The night before, Simon had fished all night in the Sea of Galilee. Have kids put their arms down at their sides and gently roll their entire bodies from side to side as if lying in the bottom of a rocking boat. **He didn't catch a thing.**

The next morning Jesus was nearby, preaching on the shore of the Sea of Galilee. Great crowds pushed against him as they tried to listen to God's Word. Have kids cross their arms and squeeze. **That wasn't going to work.**

Jesus decided to step into Simon's boat and asked Simon to push it out into the water. Have kids pretend to push a heavy boat out to water. **Then Jesus sat in the boat and taught the crowds from there so more people could hear what he had to say.** Have kids gently roll their entire bodies from side to side as if in the boat.

When he'd finished speaking, Jesus said to Simon, "Now go out where it's deeper, and let down your nets to catch some fish."

Simon was a little confused. "Master," Simon said, "we worked hard all last night and didn't catch a thing. But if you say so, I'll let the nets down again." Have kids cast their nets above their heads again, letting go of just one end. Again, have your helpers gather the ends of all the lengths of yarn and hold them tight.

And *this* **time when Simon raised his nets, they were so full of fish they began to tear!** Have kids tug gently at the yarn while you hold tight. **Simon shouted for help, and the other fishermen rowed out to give him a hand.**

When Simon realized what had happened, he fell to his knees before Jesus. Have kids clasp their hands. **His partners, James and John, the sons of Zebedee, were also amazed.**

Jesus replied to Simon, "Don't be afraid! From now on you'll be fishing for people!" And as soon as they landed, they left everything and followed Jesus. Have kids throw down their nets, and then have kids open their eyes and sit up.

13

ASK:

- What surprised you about what happened to Simon?
- Explain whether you think it's difficult or easy to obey Jesus' commands.
- What can we learn about Jesus from this Bible passage?

SAY:

Jesus has amazing power to do miracles such as this. Simon may've been tired from spending the entire night trying to catch fish; he was probably frustrated that he hadn't caught anything. So when Jesus told him to throw out his nets again, Simon probably wondered why. He'd been trying to catch fish all night and hadn't caught a thing. But Simon obeyed, and Jesus surprised him with more fish than he could fit into two boats.

ASK:

- **Tell about a time you obeyed and were glad that you did.** (Be ready with an age-appropriate example from your life of a time you obeyed and had a good result; perhaps there was a time when a parent said "Stop!" right before a car zipped past and narrowly missed you. Then encourage children to share their stories.)
- Tell which rules or directions you obey even though you don't like to obey them.
- When you love the person giving you directions, explain whether it's easier or more difficult to obey.

SAY:

Obeying isn't always the easiest or most fun thing to do, but when we obey Jesus, we can trust that he has a reason behind what he's telling us to do. Following Jesus means we obey God's Word. In fact, obeying God's Word is a way we show our love for Jesus. In John 14:15 Jesus said, "If you love me, obey my commandments."

ASK:

- Describe whether you think love and obedience go together.
- Explain when love and obedience don't go together.

14

SAY:

When we love someone, it's easier to obey what that person tells us to do. Obeying Jesus' commands is a way we show our love for him. Let's see how we can do that.

BUILD ON THE FOUNDATION

Mirror, Mirror

(about 10 minutes)

SAY:

We're going to play another game that'll help us think about what it means to obey God's Word.

Have children sit in a circle. Show kids that you have a mirror and a length of yarn or string. Ask for a willing child to go first, and have the child close his or her eyes. Gently place the string somewhere on the child where it'll be difficult to see without a mirror, such as on top of the child's head or on one shoulder. Because the string is so lightweight, the child won't likely be able to feel where you put it. Once the string is in place, have the child open his or her eyes.

SAY:

Now, let's see if our friend can guess where the string is.

The child may guess correctly, but if not, let the child use the mirror to find the string and remove it. Then let the child choose another child to take his or her place. The first child gets to place the string and the new child will guess where it is.

Play several rounds. Kids will begin to see that they can place the string very gently and the person they put it on won't be able to detect it by feel—only by use of the mirror.

ASK:

15

- Why are mirrors helpful?
- What can mirrors tell us about ourselves?

SAY:

The Bible tells us about what we just experienced.

Read aloud James 1:22-25, or ask a willing child to read it from the Bible.

ASK:

• **How is this verse like our game?**

• **How is God's Word like a "mirror" in our lives?**

SAY:

When we read the Bible, it tells us what's right and what's wrong. If we follow what the Bible tells us, we're obeying. But if we listen to God's Word and then just ignore it, it's like looking in the mirror and seeing that our hair is wacky or there's lettuce in our teeth and then not doing anything about it.

Now let's make something that'll help us remember that as Jesus' followers, we obey God's Word.

Set out markers, and give each child two large sticky notes. Kids will only use the top sticky note; the one below it will serve to protect the sticky part until kids get home to post the note they create.

SAY:

Think about what we've learned today. What would help you remember that people who follow Jesus obey God's Word, the Bible? You might want to draw a picture of Simon or a fish to remind you of how Simon obeyed even when he wasn't sure what would happen. Or you could write yourself a note that says "Take the string off your head!" as a reminder to look in the mirror of God's Word to see what you need to do. It's up to you.

Write a note to yourself or draw a simple picture. Then when you get home you can stick this on your mirror and leave it there all week as a reminder that we obey God's Word.

Allow several minutes for kids to work. As they work, you can continue the discussion about obedience, asking kids what they're creating and how it'll help them remember to obey.

When children have completed their projects,

16

SAY:

Sometimes it might seem boring or difficult to obey God's Word. But the opposite is true: When we obey God's Word, we feel joy and peace knowing that we're doing what God wants us to. Let's close our time today with a prayer.

PRAY:

Dear God, help us to look at the Bible, your Word, every day and see what you want us to do. Help us show love for you by obeying your Word. In Jesus' name, amen.

Jesus' Followers Accept God's Gifts Through Faith

Accepting God's gift of grace and love is the foundation of our relationship with Jesus and the starting point of our friendship with God. Until we recognize that Jesus died on the cross for our sins and accept this incredible gift, we won't fully know what it means to be followers of God. The same goes for your kids. Accepting Jesus' gift is based on abstract faith, and for literal-minded and practical kids, this can be tough to grasp.

This lesson will give kids hands-on experiences in trusting and accepting unwarranted gifts so they can better grasp what God's done for them. By taking away confusing language and examining God's gift to us through a simple object lesson, you'll show kids how easy it is to become Jesus' followers. You can help kids embark on their relationship with Jesus and look to build on that foundation for the rest of their lives.

Scripture Foundation

JOHN 17:7-8
Jesus prays for his disciples.

EPHESIANS 2:4-9
Paul explains that we're saved by grace because of God's love.

THIS LESSON AT A GLANCE

SEQUENCE	EXPERIENCES	SUPPLIES
SET THE FOUNDATION (about 10 minutes)	***Grateful Gifts*** Kids choose to accept or reject a gift based on its outward appearance.	• 1 mini or fun-size candy bar per child • fancy wrapping paper • small bow • transparent tape • scissors • pieces of scrap paper, each large enough to wrap a small candy bar • basket large enough to hold all the wrapped candy bars
PRESENT THE BIBLE FOUNDATION (about 25 minutes)	***Gift Wrap*** Kids explore what Jesus says about God's gifts to them as they respond to writing prompts and then gift wrap the message.	• several kid-friendly Bibles (preferably NLT) • 1 copy per child of the "Gift Box" handout (at the end of this lesson) • pens • 1 pair of scissors per child • transparent tape
BUILD ON THE FOUNDATION (about 10 minutes)	***Tie It With a Bow*** Kids write on ribbon and then use the ribbon to decorate their gift boxes as they thank God for the gifts he gives.	• fine-tipped markers • curling ribbon, 3/8-inch size • 1 pair of scissors per child • transparent tape • reflective music and music player (optional)

Before the Lesson

SET THE FOUNDATION: *GRATEFUL GIFTS*—Wrap a mini or fun-size candy bar for each child. Neatly wrap one candy bar in fancy wrapping paper and add a bow. Wrap the rest of the candy bars individually inside scrunched-up pieces of scrap paper.

PRESENT THE BIBLE FOUNDATION: *GIFT WRAP*—Copy the "Gift Box" handout, enlarging it to 122 percent. Use card stock, if desired, or you can use regular paper.

BUILD ON THE FOUNDATION: *TIE IT WITH A BOW*—Cut the curling ribbon into 12-inch lengths. You'll need five lengths per child.

20

Grateful Gifts

(about 10 minutes)

Welcome children, and have them sit in a circle.

**ALLERGY
ALERT**

See page 8.

ASK:

• **Tell about the best gift you've ever received.**

SAY:

Today I have a gift for each of you. It may not be the best gift you've ever received, but I chose these gifts with you in mind. You can decide whether to take the gift or not; it's up to you.

Show kids the gift wrapped in fancy paper and then all the other gifts wrapped in scrap paper, and then place all the gifts in a basket.

ASK:

• **Explain which gift you'd prefer—and why.**

Offer a gift from the basket to each child one at a time, including the nicely wrapped gift. As you do, remind kids that you chose the gifts for them and you think the gifts are special. Allow each child the option to choose to accept or reject the gift, and then move on to the next child. After offering a gift to everyone, let the kids who chose to accept a gift unwrap theirs.

ASK:

• **Explain what it was like to accept your gift based on its outward appearance.**
• **Now that you know what the gift is, explain whether you wish you'd chosen differently.**

Let kids who didn't accept a gift take one, and then have everyone enjoy their treats together.

SAY:

When you couldn't tell what the gift was based on its wrapping, you had to trust me when I told you you'd like it. God has gifts for you, too.

21

And just as you had to trust me that my gifts were good, the Bible tells us to trust God and accept his gifts through faith. Let's learn more about what the Bible says about God's gifts for us.

PRESENT THE BIBLE FOUNDATION

Gift Wrap

(about 25 minutes)

SAY:
One place the Bible talks about the gifts God has for us is in a prayer from Jesus. Let's check it out.

Read aloud John 17:7-8.

While praying, Jesus told God that his disciples knew that everything Jesus had was a gift from God.

ASK:
- **Explain what gifts you think Jesus is talking about in this passage.**
- **Why do you think it's important that Jesus told his disciples about his gifts from God?**

Then read Ephesians 2:4-9 aloud to the kids.

ASK:
- **Describe some gifts God has given you.**
- **According to this passage, why do you think Jesus gave these gifts to you?**

SAY:
Let's think some more about what these verses mean.

Encourage kids to spread out around the room. Give each child scissors, a pen, and a copy of the "Gift Box" handout. Instruct kids to carefully cut out the gift box on the solid lines.

22

Ask kids to spend time thinking about each phrase on the handout and then write down a short phrase based on what they've learned from the verses and what they know about God through their relationship with him. Be ready with examples for each phrase. Encourage kids to look back at Scriptures discussed in their Bibles if they need more direction.

After a few minutes, gather kids back together and demonstrate how to create the finished gift box. Make a crease along each dashed line, and then show kids how to tape each small folded lip to the back of the unattached square next to it so the words face inward. Continue taping each section until you've created a cube minus the bottom of the box. (The bottom remains open so kids can look inside and remember what they wrote in response to these verses.)

ASK:
- **What kinds of things did you write about on your gift box?**
- **Explain why you have or haven't accepted these gifts God has for you.**

SAY:
God's greatest gift to us is his Son, Jesus. God sent Jesus as a gift to us—to die for us—so we can be free of sin and death forever. When we believe that Jesus died on the cross for us and accept God's incredible gift, we become followers of God. We can accept God's gifts through faith. Let's thank God for his amazing gifts to us.

BUILD ON THE FOUNDATION

Tie It With a Bow

(about 10 minutes)

Give each child a fine-tipped marker and five strips of curling ribbon.

23

SAY:

Jesus is God's greatest gift to us. To follow Jesus, we have to accept this amazing gift through faith.

ASK:

• **Describe other gifts God has given us.** (Along with practical necessities, encourage kids to think about the spiritual gifts God's given them, such as love, joy, and peace.)

Ask kids to write one gift God has given them on each strip of the curling ribbon. Allow time.

Then show kids how to carefully run a ribbon along the sharpened edge of open scissors. Explain to kids that they'll curl each one of their ribbons. As they curl each ribbon, encourage kids to silently say, "God, thank you for the gift of [name what's written on the ribbon]." You may want to quietly play reflective music in the background while kids talk to God.

Give kids tape. Ask kids to continue to talk privately to God as they tape each ribbon to the top of their gift boxes from the previously activity. As they tape each ribbon, encourage kids to silently say, "God I accept your gift of…[name what's written on the ribbon]."

PRAY:

Dear God, you've given us more than we can ever understand or deserve. Help us to accept through faith the gift of Jesus' sacrifice and every other good and perfect gift you give us. Thank you for loving us! In Jesus' name, amen.

LEADER TIP

Kids may want to accept God's gift of Jesus' sacrifice as a result of this lesson. If you have a child who shows interest or has questions, talk with the child and follow your ministry's guidelines for walking a child through this life-changing commitment.

GIFT BOX

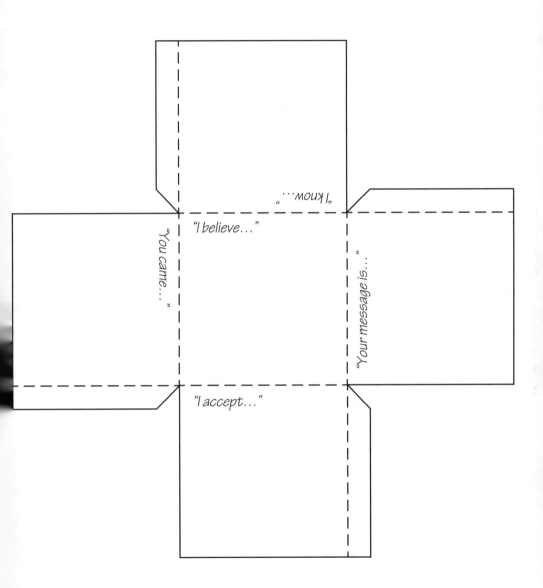

"I believe…"

"I know…"

"You came…"

"Your message is…"

"I accept…"

Permission to photocopy this page from *13 Most Important Bible Lessons for Kids About Living for Jesus* granted for local church use. Copyright © Group Publishing, Inc., 1515 Cascade Ave., Loveland, CO 80538. group.com

LESSON 2: Jesus' Followers Accept God's Gifts Through Faith

Jesus' Followers Belong to God

N o one likes to be left out, but kids especially are searching for where they belong in their world: Which people do they belong with, what activities are they good at, and where do they fit in at school? This lesson is a powerful reminder to kids that, no matter what happens around them or to them, they belong to God. And with the knowledge that they belong to God, kids have a built-in relief valve for the pressure of trying to fit in everywhere else. As kids decide to put their faith in Jesus, they can trust that they're always precious and special to God. They'll discover that their meaning and worth comes from belonging to God rather than belonging to that crowd or being in that club. As you help your kids discover what it means to belong to God, you'll transform how they think and feel about themselves.

Scripture Foundation

JOHN 17:9
Jesus talks to God about his disciples belonging to God.

DEUTERONOMY 7:6-8
Belonging to God makes us his special treasure.

1 JOHN 3:7-10
John explains that our actions show who we belong to.

THIS LESSON AT A GLANCE

SEQUENCE	EXPERIENCES	SUPPLIES
SET THE FOUNDATION (about 10 minutes)	***Match-Up*** Kids attempt to correctly match an item to its owner.	• black trash bag
PRESENT THE BIBLE FOUNDATION (about 25 minutes)	***Left Out*** In pairs, kids discuss questions based on the Bible verse and discover what it's like to not belong.	• kid-friendly Bible (preferably NLT)
BUILD ON THE FOUNDATION (about 10 minutes)	***Give It Up*** Kids respond physically to prayer prompts as they think about how belonging to God affects them.	• reflective music and music player (optional)

Match-Up

(about 10 minutes)

Greet kids as they enter the room, and ask them individually to remove one of their belongings, such as a shoe, sock, or trinket and place it in the black trash bag so others can't see. Do your best to keep kids from seeing what others place in the bag.

Have kids sit in a circle.

SAY:

Inside this bag, there's something that belongs to each of you. You'll each get to reach in without looking, choose an item, and try to guess who it belongs to. If you correctly match the belonging to the person, return the item to that person. If you guess incorrectly, return the item to the bag and pass the bag to the next person. Hand the bag to one child. **Ready? Go!**

Play until every person is correctly matched with a belonging.

ASK:

- **Describe what helped you decide which item belonged to which person.**
- **When we say something "belongs to you," explain what you think that means.**
- **Tell about your most important belonging.**

SAY:

Your belongings usually say something about you. You might be kind of spunky, so you like to wear wild socks. Or maybe your dress shoes tell us it's important to you to dress up for church. What belongs to you is usually also important to you. You take better care of something when it's yours. You might write your name on your belongings in case they get lost. You look for your belongings when they're missing. And you worry about them when you can't find them. Today we're going to discover what the Bible says about belonging to God. Let's check it out.

29

Left Out

(about 25 minutes)

SAY:

In the Bible passage we're about to discuss, Jesus is talking to God in prayer. Let's read what Jesus said to God.

Read aloud John 17:9.

ASK:

- **What do you think it means that you've been given to Jesus?**
- **Explain what you think it means to belong to God.**
- **What do you think it says about God that we belong to him?**

Read aloud Deuteronomy 7:6-8.

ASK:

- **What do you think it means to be God's "special treasure"?**
- **Think of your most precious belonging. Explain whether or not you'd describe it as a "special treasure."**
- **Why do you think this Bible passage refers to us as something so special to God?**

SAY:

Let's play a game to help us think more about what it means to belong—and what it means to be left out. We'll experience what it's like to be left out.

Have kids race to find a partner; you'll need to either join in or stay out of the game to ensure an odd number of kids are playing. Once all but one of the kids have a partner, ask one of the following questions. Allow one minute for kids to discuss their responses. When you say "go," kids must race to find a new partner and answer a new question. With each new pairing, one child will be left out. Ask enough questions so every child sits out at least once. Here are a few questions to get you started.

30

- **Would you rather pray for someone else or have someone pray for you?**

- Would you rather lose your ability to laugh or your ability to sleep?
- Would you rather live in a world without sunlight or in a world where it's never dark?
- Would you rather be hairy all over or have no hair at all?
- Would you rather have the super power of invisibility or of mind reading?
- Would you rather be popular but lonely or be uncool with lots of good friends?
- Would you rather belong to God or someone else?
- Would you rather have to face your worst fear or eat the grossest food on the planet?
- Would you rather meet Mary or Joseph?
- Would you rather swim in the middle of the ocean or bungee jump off a tall bridge?

Once you've played so everyone has had a turn to be without a partner, gather kids in a circle.

ASK:
- What was different when you were the one left out?
- What was it like when you had a partner and someone else was left out?
- Tell about a time you were left out in real life.

Read aloud 1 John 3:7-10.

ASK:
- What do you think belonging to God means in everyday life?
- What changes about us when we belong to God?
- Explain whether you think God leaves out anyone or if we all belong to him.

SAY:
It doesn't feel good for anyone to be left out. The good news is that God doesn't want anyone to be left out, either. We're all special and important to God. The Bible tells us that when we accept the gift Jesus gave us when he died on the cross, we belong to God. People who follow Jesus belong to God. Let's look at ways we can remember we belong to God.

31

Give It Up

(about 10 minutes)

Ask kids to spread out around the room. You may want to quietly play reflective music in the background to set the tone. Explain to kids that for each prayer prompt, they'll mimic your actions and respond silently in prayer. Repeat the prayer prompt below filling in the appropriate body part and action, and then pause for a time of silent, responsive prayer.

SAY:

God, my [body part] **belongs to you, so I will...**
Heart: Cross hands over heart; then pause.
Ears: Cover ears; then pause.
Eyes: Look toward the ceiling; then pause.
Hands: Hold out hands, palms faceup; then pause.
Mouth: Press lips tightly together; then pause.
Feet: Walk around the room; then pause.

ASK:

• **What's one thing you'll do differently this week because you know you belong to God?**

PRAY:

Dear God, thank you for choosing us and not leaving us out. Thank you for making us special and for allowing us to belong to you. Please help us make wise choices and act the way you want us to act. We love you! In Jesus' name, amen.

32

LESSON 4

Jesus' Followers Bring Glory to Jesus

When children dream of playing major league baseball, lighting up the silver screen, serving as president of the United States, or being a much-loved parent—they're dreaming of glory. It's human nature to yearn for the glory of achieving goals and earning recognition for achievements. Jesus, on the other hand, didn't need to do anything at all to achieve glory. He is glorious and deserves to be glorified. And yet—Jesus did more for us than we could ever do for ourselves when he died to save us from sin and reunite us with God. Our Savior deserves more praise than we can offer in our lifetime. In this lesson, kids will understand that everything they are and do can bring glory to Jesus.

Scripture Foundation

JOHN 17:10, 14
Jesus tells God that his people bring him glory because God gives them to Jesus.

PSALM 44:8
We can give glory to God.

PHILIPPIANS 1:11
Jesus fills our lives with goodness, and we in turn bring glory to him.

1 PETER 4:10-11
We can use the gifts God gives us to bring him glory.

REVELATION 4:11
Jesus is worthy to receive glory.

THIS LESSON AT A GLANCE

SEQUENCE	EXPERIENCES	SUPPLIES
SET THE FOUNDATION (about 10 minutes)	***Yay, You!*** Kids cheer each other for who they are and what they do.	• none
PRESENT THE BIBLE FOUNDATION (about 25 minutes)	***Yay, Jesus!*** Kids discover what the Bible says about how they can glorify Jesus.	• kid-friendly Bibles (preferably NLT) • paper • pens and markers • a variety of craft supplies for kids to choose from • 2 pieces of paper, 1 labeled "Philippians 1:11" and 1 labeled "1 Peter 4:10-11" • transparent tape
BUILD ON THE FOUNDATION (about 10 minutes)	***Yay, All Life Long!*** Kids spend time in worship to bring glory to Jesus.	• large sheet of paper with Revelation 4:11 written out • marker • transparent tape

Before the Lesson

BUILD ON THE FOUNDATION: *YAY, ALL LIFE LONG!* —On a large sheet of paper, write "You are worthy, O Lord our God, to receive glory and honor and power" (Revelation 4:11).

Yay, You!

(about 10 minutes)

Greet kids, and ask them to sit in a circle with you.

SAY:

Please close your eyes. Now think of something you did once that was nice, helpful, or maybe even heroic. Keep your eyes closed and imagine yourself in that situation. Think specifically about what you did that was so great. Pause for a few seconds so kids can think.

Let's hear your stories. You'll each tell us what you did—and act it out in 10 seconds. For example, if you saved a dog from drowning, then pretend you're wading through water holding the dog. In response, we will explode in five seconds of wild praise for you.

Practice cheering (and stopping) a few times for fun. Then start with the person on your left. After the child has acted out the situation, direct the rest of the group to cheer for five seconds. Ensure every child has a chance to act and be cheered for.

ASK:

- **Explain what it was like when others cheered for you.**
- **Tell about a time you cheered wildly for someone.**
- **Why do you think we give praise to people when they do great things, but not for just being who they are?**

SAY:

There's a difference between being praised for what we do and simply being appreciated for who we are. Let's try this again. We'll go around the circle again. This time all you'll do is complete this sentence: "I am [name]." And we're going to cheer for you for five seconds—just for being you.

Go around the circle the opposite direction and lead kids in cheering for each other.

35

ASK:

- How did this time around the circle feel different from the first time?
- Explain whether you think it's important to appreciate people just for who they are.

SAY:

Not everyone likes to be the center of attention, but we all like to do things well and feel appreciated. Here's my appreciation for you: You're all amazing people and I'm grateful to be with you today. It's great to hear about the things you've done, too. We can appreciate everyone here for who we are and the things we've done.

When we cheer for each other, we're giving each other what the Bible calls *glory*. That means we're praising each other for what we do and who we are. People who follow Jesus bring glory to him. Psalm 44:8 says, "O God, we give glory to you all day long and constantly praise your name." Jesus deserves glory because he's God—so good, so loving, so incredibly more amazing than anything we can imagine. And Jesus deserves glory because he died on the cross to save us from sin and bring us back to God, who loves us so much. Let's talk more about bringing glory to Jesus.

PRESENT THE BIBLE FOUNDATION

Yay, Jesus!

(about 25 minutes)

Gather your group on one side of your room.

SAY:

I'm going to read to you sentences from a prayer that Jesus prayed to God. While I read, I'll direct you to move to different parts of the room to act out this prayer together. The other side of the room represents

God. The middle of the room represents the world. And I'll represent Jesus. Ready? Here's what Jesus said in John 17:10 and 14:

All who are mine *(extend your arms to indicate the group)*
belong to you, *(send the group to the other side of the room)*
and you have given them to me, *(bring the group back to you)*
so they bring me glory. *(ask kids to raise their hands toward heaven)*
I have given them your word. *(send them back to God)*
And the world *(ask them to come to the middle of the room and cower as if someone's against them)* **hates them because they do not belong to the world,**
just as I *(join the group in the middle of the room, but stand tall)*
do not belong to the world. *(invite the group to stand tall with you, arms raised over their heads in victory)*

ASK:
- **What do you think it means to give glory to Jesus in real life?**
- **What do you think Jesus meant when he said the world "hates" us?**
- **Tell about a time you experienced hate from the world because you follow Jesus.** (Be ready with your own example.)
- **Describe Jesus' prayer in your own words.**

SAY:
Jesus said we bring him glory because God gave us to him. That can be difficult to understand because our actions aren't always full of glory. Let's look at the Bible for clues about how we can bring glory to Jesus.

Form two groups, and have them move to opposite sides of the room. Give each group a Bible, and give one group the piece of paper with Philippians 1:11 written on it and the other group the piece of paper with 1 Peter 4:10-11 written on it. Have groups read their corresponding Bible passages.

SAY:
Once you've read the passage, discuss how you think it relates to how you live your life to bring glory to Jesus. Then get ready with your group to teach your passage to the other group. You can rewrite the passage in your own words, come up with a main point and set it to a tune, illustrate it, put together a simple skit to show what the passage would look like—whatever you choose. Remember: The goal is to bring

37

glory to Jesus as you work. You'll have several minutes before you present to the rest of us.

Set out the paper, pens, markers, and craft supplies for kids to use if they choose. As groups work, circulate to answer any questions kids may have. After several minutes, ask each group to take turns presenting what the Bible says.

ASK:
- **What did you learn about how we bring glory to Jesus?**
- **What, if anything, surprised you about ways we can bring glory to Jesus?**

Give each group a piece of paper and a marker, and have them choose someone to be the Recorder.

SAY:
Now we'll swap passages. For the Philippians group, you'll brainstorm a list of qualities that you think describe Jesus and his followers. For the First Peter group, you'll brainstorm a list of gifts and talents you think God gives people. You have five minutes. Ready? Go!

When time's up, tape the two papers where everyone can see them. Have everyone sit in a circle again.

SAY:
Take a look at the Philippians page. It contains a list of qualities of who we are as followers of Jesus. Choose one you'd like to focus on this week. For example, let's say you want to live with more kindness. After you've chosen a quality, take a look at the First Peter page and choose a gift or talent you think applies to you. If you don't see one, you can come up with your own. Allow time.

Now we'll go around the circle as everyone completes this sentence: "I glorify Jesus by being [name the quality].**"**

Once you've gone around the entire circle, repeat the experience with this sentence: **"I glorify Jesus with my gift of** [name the gift or talent].**"**

Afterward, **SAY:**
God created us wonderfully, and when we love and follow Jesus he creates good qualities in our lives. God's given us good abilities, gifts, and talents we can use to glorify him. Everything we are and everything we do can glorify Jesus as we live our lives for him.

38

Yay, All Life Long!

(about 10 minutes)

SAY:

Turn to someone near you and describe what you've learned so far about glorifying Jesus and what you can do personally to bring glory to Jesus. Allow time.

People who follow Jesus bring glory to Jesus through who they are and what they do. One of the important ways we glorify Jesus is by spending time worshipping him.

ASK:

• How do you think worship brings glory to Jesus?

Tape the paper with Revelation 4:11 written out where everyone can see it.

SAY:

Think back to our activity when we cheered for each other. When we spend time worshipping Jesus, it's kind of like cheering for him. Let's read this verse from the book of Revelation together, saying the words directly to Jesus. Let's read: "You are worthy, O Lord our God, to receive glory and honor and power."

Repeat the verse once or twice more.

SAY:

Now let's pray this verse quietly in our minds and hearts. Repeat it twice as you imagine Jesus standing before you.

Allow time.

SAY:

Now let's pray this verse in a round. Designate half the circle as one group and the other half as another group. **We'll start with one group saying the first phrase—"You are worthy"—and the next group saying the second phrase—"O Lord our God"—and the first group saying the last phrase—**

39

"to receive glory and honor and power." We'll go back and forth until we've said the phrase four times. Remember—we're praying and bringing glory to Jesus.

Direct the prayer time so kids start out quiet, get louder, louder still, and then quiet again. Then ask kids to bow their heads in prayer.

PRAY:

Dear Jesus, you are worthy to receive glory and honor and power. Thank you for being our Lord. Thank you for loving us so much that you died to save us. Thank you for creating good qualities in us so that we can be more like you. Thank you for giving us gifts, talents, and abilities so that everything we are and everything we do brings glory to you. Help us to be the people you've created us to be and do the things you've created us to do so that we always bring glory to you. In your name, amen.

LESSON 5

Jesus' Followers Live in the World but Aren't of It

The children you serve don't live in one world; they live in several. There are the worlds of school, home, and church; the world they create with their friends; the worlds they visit online. Each of those worlds has its own rules and demands, and children are quick to adapt as they shift between worlds. Today you'll help children discover that, no matter which world they're in, first and foremost they're followers of Jesus, citizens of the kingdom of God. That's the world that lasts forever, the world that's their true home.

Scripture Foundation

JOHN 17:11
Jesus says his followers are in the world, but not of the world.

PSALM 119:105
We spend time with God.

LUKE 4:4
We can know what God wants us to do by reading his Word.

2 PETER 1:1-3
We can rely on Jesus' power.

EPHESIANS 6:11
We're serious about following Jesus.

GALATIANS 2:20
We're not the same people we were.

1 THESSALONIANS 5:11
It's important to spend time with other people who follow Jesus.

2 TIMOTHY 3:14
We stay faithful to what God's Word teaches us.

THIS LESSON AT A GLANCE

SEQUENCE	EXPERIENCES	SUPPLIES
SET THE FOUNDATION (about 10 minutes)	***Name Tag News*** Kids fill out their name tags with their names and the roles they have in life on earth.	• self-adhesive name tags • markers • pens
PRESENT THE BIBLE FOUNDATION (about 25 minutes)	***Living the Life*** Kids dig into the Bible and consider how to remember that they're not of this world due to their faith in Jesus.	• several kid-friendly Bibles (preferably NLT) • 1 raw egg, plus an extra • copies of the "Bible References" handout (at the end of this lesson) • scissors • pens • paper • marker • poster board or whiteboard • bowl of water and paper towels for cleanup (optional)
BUILD ON THE FOUNDATION (about 10 minutes)	***Name Tags Revisited*** Kids fill out second name tags and place them over their existing name tags as a reminder that our faith in Jesus means a new identity.	• kid-friendly Bible (preferably NLT) • self-adhesive name tags • pens

Before the Lesson

SET THE FOUNDATION: *NAME TAG NEWS*— Place name tags and markers where kids can write as they enter the room. Have pens available to distribute later.

PRESENT THE BIBLE FOUNDATION: *LIVING THE LIFE*— Make copies of the "Bible References" handout and cut apart strips so each group will have one or more strips.

42

Name Tag News

(about 10 minutes)

Welcome kids as they arrive, and ask them to write their name on a name tag with a marker. Tell them not to peel the backs off the name tags.

Once everyone's done, gather kids in a circle and give each child a pen.

SAY:

Thanks for filling out your name tags. It's nice to know your name, but your name alone doesn't tell me much about you.

Let's turn our name tags into "news tags" by adding more information about who we are in the world we live in.

Write words that describe you on your name tag in response to the questions I ask. Use small writing, because you'll be describing yourself in lots of ways!

Pause for a few seconds after each question to allow kids time to write.

If you have parents, write "son" or "daughter."

If you go to school, write "student."

If you like to play a sport, write "athlete" or the name of your sport.

If there are other kids in your family, write "brother" or "sister."

If you like to sing, write, or draw, write "singer," "writer," or "artist."

If you have a grandparent, write "grandson" or "granddaughter."

If you like to create stuff, write "creative."

If you like to swim, write "swimmer."

If you have a pet, write "pet owner."

If you like to read, write "reader."

If you have friends, write "friend."

If you like to search for stuff online, write "explorer."

If you have a hobby, write the name of your hobby.

SAY:

Now you have very full name tags because you have very full lives! Let's talk about what you wrote.

43

ASK:

- Describe one word on your name tag that makes you happy, and why.
- Choose two things on your name tag that would be hard to do at the same time, and explain why.

Ask kids to put on their name tags.

SAY:

It would be difficult to swim and write a story at the same time. And if you tried singing and swimming at the same time you might have a challenge.

But you can be a pet owner, student, and a grandchild all at the same time. And no matter what you're doing, or where you are, you never stop being you.

You're *always* you.

And something else stays the same no matter where you are or what you're doing: If you follow Jesus, that doesn't change either. If you follow Jesus, you follow him when you're at home, at school, playing sports, with friends...always.

You live *in* this world, but you're not *of* this world.

Let's dig into the Bible and discover exactly what that means.

PRESENT THE BIBLE FOUNDATION

Living the Life

(about 25 minutes)

SAY:

When Jesus was about to return to heaven, he was in a room with his closest followers, the disciples. He prayed for them.

Ask a willing child to read aloud John 17:11.

SAY:

Jesus knew he was leaving his followers behind, but he wanted them to stick together and be faithful even when tough times came because he knew that the world—culture, events, and society all around them—wouldn't treat his friends very well. Jesus wanted his disciples to be focused on him and not what was happening in the world. He wanted them to be in the world, but not of the world.

Tough times were coming—very soon.

Within a few days, Jesus was arrested and died on a cross. Jesus' followers thought they might be arrested, too, and went into hiding. They were scared and confused.

And all the disciples' promises about following Jesus were crowded out by those feelings of fear and confusion.

So much for staying faithful. When pressure came, their faithfulness broke like a fragile eggshell.

Hold up a raw egg.

SAY:

This is a raw egg. If I drop it, what do you think will happen?

Pause for kids to answer. Assure kids that it is indeed a raw egg and not one that's been hardboiled.

Eggs break easily and they make a mess!

Stand over a child, and hold the egg inches above his or her head.

Raise your hand when you think the egg is high enough that, if I drop it, it'll break.

SAY:

Like this fragile eggshell can easily break, the harsh reality of the world, or events and culture around us, can cause our faithfulness to break. Jesus knew the world would be a hard place for his followers to live in. It can be harsh and unforgiving. But Jesus wants us to remember that God is always loving and forgiving.

When we're too focused on who we are and what's happening in this world, we can forget about our faithfulness to Jesus and let our faith become fragile. Set aside the egg.

45

ASK:

- Describe some of the things in this world that can make our faith fragile.
- Why do you think Jesus wants us to keep our focus on him rather than on this world?
- What do you think it means to be in the world but not of it?

SAY:

Being in the world but not of it means that we're not tied to what the world around us says is important, but instead we live for what God says is important. The Bible gives us great advice on how to faithfully follow Jesus and do what God wants us to do—no matter what's going on in the world around us. Let's see what the Bible tells us.

Form small groups (two kids can be a small group), and give each group one or more of the "Bible References" strips. Also give each group a Bible, pen, and piece of paper. Ask each group to look up and read the assigned passages and then be ready to summarize to the larger group what they read. Encourage groups to use the table of contents in the Bible as needed to help find each passage. The Scripture references are listed here for your convenience:

- Psalm 119:105
- Luke 4:4
- 2 Peter 1:1-3
- Ephesians 6:11
- Galatians 2:20
- 1 Thessalonians 5:11
- 2 Timothy 3:14

Allow about five minutes for kids to read and come up with a summary of their passages. Then ask groups to read aloud the passages they were assigned and describe what they think they mean. Write notes about what kids have to say about each passage on a piece of poster board or on a whiteboard where everyone can see.

SAY:

This is all good advice—but we don't always follow it.

ASK:

- Explain which advice you think is easiest to follow, and why.
- Explain which advice is the most difficult to follow, and why.

SAY:

God gives us the strength and power to be faithful to Jesus and to keep our faith strong. But we have to rely on God and not the world around us. God transforms us—and helps us be faithful no matter what's happening in the world. God helps us handle pressure and distractions, and we can trust him.

I'll show you how we can keep our faith in God strong.

Have kids sit in a circle on the floor, and hold up the egg.

We won't see how far the egg can drop without breaking. Instead, let's find out how hard you can squeeze it before it breaks.

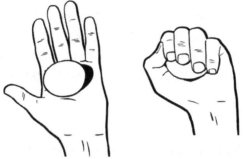

Demonstrate holding the egg as shown. Hold out one hand, and then place the egg in your palm. Close your hand around the egg so all your fingers are completely wrapped around it. Squeeze, applying pressure evenly around the egg. No matter how hard you squeeze, the even pressure applied will prevent the egg from breaking.

SAY:

I want you all to take turns squeezing this egg. You'll hold it the way I'm holding it and squeeze the way I'm squeezing it. Please closely follow my example.

Remind kids to open their palm, wrap their fingers completely around the egg, and then squeeze. Let all the kids take turns squeezing the egg as you've demonstrated. Help kids position their fingers, if necessary, and hold your hands under theirs to avoid an accidental drop.

SAY:

What's weak can become strong in the right hands. When we place ourselves in God's hands—all day, every day, everywhere we go, and no matter what's happening in the world around us—our faith can grow strong, too.

With God's help, we can keep our faith strong and our focus on him.

47

Name Tags Revisited

(about 10 minutes)

Ask kids to find a partner.

SAY:

Tell your partner which of the roles on your name tag is where you find it difficult to stay focused on Jesus. For instance, when you're playing sports maybe you find it hard to control your temper and you forget about following Jesus. Maybe you start throwing words and elbows.

Allow time.

ASK:

- **Explain why you think it can be difficult to stay focused on God when we live in this world.**
- **From our last activity, which piece of advice from the Bible do you think could help you when you have a hard time staying focused on Jesus?**
- **Explain how following God can help us be in the world but not of it.**

Allow time, and then give another name tag to each child. Ask kids to write their name and "Not of This World" on their new name tag. Then they can place the new tag over the old tag they're wearing.

Read aloud John 17:11.

SAY:

Jesus prayed for all of his disciples—even ones who hadn't been born yet. That means you and me, too. He wants us to stick together, stay focused on what he says is important, and be faithful—and he'll help us do that.

No matter where you are or what you're doing in this world, you can stay focused on God and on being in the world but not of it. God wants us to stay focused on what he says is important and not be distracted by what the world says is important. He wants us to rely on him to keep our

48

faith strong. He wants us to look to the Bible, his Word, to help us not be of the world. God wants us to be focused on him no matter where we are in this world—school, your home, your friendships, everywhere. I'm glad we can stick together and encourage each other, no matter what's happening in the world around us. We can always be encouraged to stay focused on God. God helps us not be of the world. Let's pray for each other now.

Ask kids to stand next to their partner.

PRAY:

Dear God, thank you for walking with us everywhere we go and for being with us no matter what we're doing. Help us be your faithful followers, God. Please help us remember to stay focused on you always, so that we may be in the world but not of it. Thank you for our friends and for letting us be your friend. In Jesus' name, amen.

Bible References

Psalm 119:105

Luke 4:4

2 Peter 1:1-3

Ephesians 6:11

Galatians 2:20

1 Thessalonians 5:11

2 Timothy 3:14

Permission to photocopy this page from *13 Most Important Bible Lessons for Kids About Living for Jesus* granted for local church use. Copyright © Group Publishing, Inc., 1515 Cascade Ave., Loveland, CO 80538. group.com

LESSON 6

Jesus' Followers Trust in God's Protection

It can be tough to be a kid. There are grownups to please and, perhaps, to fear. You're small in a large world, unable to control where you live, where you go, maybe even what you eat for dinner. You're vulnerable and the world has a way of reminding you of that—often. Yet Jesus promises that God will protect us—especially the smallest among us—and he does, though not always in the ways we might expect. This promise can be difficult for a child to reconcile when parents are divorcing or a grandparent dies. As you gently lead kids in exploring and understanding this promise, you'll help them discover that while life comes with bumps and bruises, they have God's love and protection always—even until they join him in eternity.

Scripture Foundation

JOHN 17:12
Jesus protects us.

JOHN 10:27-29
We're protected by God, and nothing can change that.

2 CORINTHIANS 12:6-7
Our health isn't always protected.

JOHN 16:32-33
Even people who follow Jesus face troubles.

2 CORINTHIANS 12:8-10
We are weak.

MATTHEW 5:11-12
People may be mean to us.

HEBREWS 9:27-28
Our physical lives will end.

ROMANS 8:28-30, 35, 37-39
Our struggles and problems lead to a good end with God.

THIS LESSON AT A GLANCE

SEQUENCE	EXPERIENCES	SUPPLIES
SET THE FOUNDATION (about 10 minutes)	***Superheroes*** Kids draw or write about what their preferred superhero power is.	• 1 plain white paper plate per child • pens or pencils
PRESENT THE BIBLE FOUNDATION (about 25 minutes)	***A Promise Kept?*** Kids explore whether God is keeping his promise to protect his people and if so, how.	• 5 kid-friendly Bibles (preferably NLT) • pens • 1 copy of the "Bible References" handout (at the end of this lesson) • scissors
BUILD ON THE FOUNDATION (about 10 minutes)	***Yours Forever*** Kids discover how God protects them and pray for God's protection.	• kid-friendly Bible (preferably NLT)

Before the Lesson

PRESENT THE BIBLE FOUNDATION: *A PROMISE KEPT?* — Cut apart the copy you made of the "Bible References" handout so each of five groups will have one strip. Also, be ready with a personal example of a difficult time you've faced that later you could see God using for good.

Superheroes

(about 10 minutes)

Welcome kids, and give each child a paper plate and a pen or pencil.

SAY:

Congratulations—you're all getting a promotion!

You are now officially superheroes. The question is: What's your special superhero power and how will you use it to help people?

As for me, if I could become a superhero, I'd want the power of...

Describe what superpower you'd want and how you'd use it to help others. Then ask kids to draw or write on their plates the one superpower they'd choose so they could help others, such as invisibility to do good deeds or ultra strength to rescue people in danger.

Allow about two minutes; then have kids sit in a circle.

SAY:

Now we'll take turns striking a superhero pose and telling about your one power and how you'd use it to help others. Remember—superheroes stand tall with shoulders back, heads up, capes blowing in the wind.

Go around the circle letting each child have a chance to talk.

SAY:

Thanks for letting us know your superpower. Now let's put all of your superpowers to the test to see if you'll be able to protect people—no matter what.

Please stand and strike your superhero pose *only* if your one superpower can protect people in these situations:

Pause after each scenario for kids to respond.

- **An asteroid is about to hit earth and end all life on the planet.**
- **A cat is stuck in a tree.**
- **A kid is about to sneeze and give everyone in class his cold.**
- **Someone has cancer and is dying.**
- **A dog is about to bite a little girl on the playground.**

53

- Parents of a friend are about to get a divorce.
- Two of your friends are angry with each other and fighting.
- Someone stole your friend's bike and he's spending every second searching to get it back.
- Your computer crashed and won't start again.

Allow time.

SAY:

Thanks for helping where you can, superheroes.

ASK:

- **What superpower would you need to fix all the problems we talked about?**

SAY:

Even superheroes can't fix every problem. As much as we like to admire superheroes, the truth is we can't trust them to protect us from everything that can happen in life.

God isn't a superhero; he's something even greater. God promises in the Bible that he can—and will—protect us. Let's see how God keeps that promise.

PRESENT THE BIBLE FOUNDATION

A Promise Kept?

(about 25 minutes)

Read aloud John 17:12.

SAY:

As Jesus prayed, he indicated that he's counting on God to protect his followers. When Jesus says this, he echoes other places in the Bible that tell us we can trust God to work for our good.

Listen to this…

Ask a willing child to read aloud John 10:27-29.

Jesus promises to protect us, and we can trust what he says. But in what ways are we protected? Will God keep us safe if a tornado or hurricane hits our town? Or if we get really sick? Or if a bully comes after us?

Let's talk about that.

ASK:

- **Explain whether you think God keeps us safe in every way—and why or why not.**
- **Tell about a time God kept you safe.**

SAY:

In addition to being superheroes, you're detectives now. See whether God promises to protect us in every way possible.

Form up to five groups, and ask groups to move apart in the room so they can talk freely without distracting each other. Give each group a Bible, a pen, and one of the "Bible References" strips. Ask groups to look up their passage (encourage them to use the Bible's table of contents as needed to find their passage). They'll read the passage and then discuss their question. When you call time, each group will report back to the larger group. The Scripture references and questions are listed here for your convenience:

- 2 Corinthians 12:6-7: Explain whether God promises to always protect our health.
- John 16:32-33: Explain whether God promises to protect us from having trouble.
- 2 Corinthians 12:8-10: Explain whether God always protects us from weakness.
- Matthew 5:11-12: Explain whether God always protects us from bullies.
- Hebrews 9:27-28: Explain whether God always protects us from dying.

Allow up to five minutes for groups to work. Then bring groups back together, and have each group read aloud its assigned passage and then answer the question. Ask groups to report back in the order listed. After each group reports, ask everyone:

- **Explain whether you agree or disagree with what this group said.**

SAY:

God promises to protect us—but we still experience sickness, trouble, weakness, bullies, and dying. If we still experience those things, it's easy to wonder how God protects us.

We can depend on God to protect us by always being here for us and

55

by always working for our good—*especially* when we experience bad or sad things. And we can trust that when those things happen, God is always with us.

Ask a willing child to read aloud Romans 8:28-30.

Sometimes when bad things happen, we can start to think that God has left us. But God's still here—always—working to make good things happen for us even when we face hard times.

Once, I faced a difficult situation that turned out for good when...

Share your age-appropriate personal example.

SAY:

We can't always see it, we don't always feel it, things don't always turn out the way we want them to—but God is always in charge. He knows the bigger picture of our lives when we don't. So even during bad experiences, we can have faith that God is always working for our good.

God protects us, and he uses our experiences for our ultimate good. Let's think about how we can embrace that kind of protection in our lives.

BUILD ON THE FOUNDATION

Yours Forever

(about 10 minutes)

SAY:

Sometimes we ask God to heal someone we love or help us in school. Sometimes God steps in to fix what's broken or give us a hand, but he doesn't promise that bad and sad things won't happen in our lives. No matter what's happening around us, God protects us in ways we may not see or feel.

56

ASK:

- Explain why you think bad things still happen to us if God protects us.
- Tell about a time something bad or sad was happening in your life and you could sense God's protection.

SAY:

God most likely won't fly in like a superhero to rescue you when bad things are going on in your life. Instead, we can have faith in God's promise in the Bible: God always protects us by working for our ultimate good.

Read aloud Romans 8:35, 37-39.

SAY:

Jesus' love is forever and is bigger than anything we'll ever face. It's even bigger than our death. When we know and follow Jesus, we can look forward to life forever in heaven with him.

It's almost certain we'll run into trouble here on earth. And it can be hard to understand why. It can be difficult to understand how God is protecting us when bad things are happening, but he's always here with us.

I love that Jesus protects me in a way no superhero ever could.

Ask kids to stand.

SAY:

We all chose cool superpowers so we could protect people. But even our superpowers can't help everyone all the time.

Strike your superhero poses for me again, please.

Join kids in a striking a superhero pose.

SAY:

If your superpower is to love everyone no matter what and give anyone who follows you life forever, stay standing. Otherwise, sit back down.

Allow time for kids to be seated.

SAY:

When we follow Jesus, we can trust in God's protection—forever. Now let's tell Jesus where we could use his protection in our lives right

57

now. He may not always take away our troubles, but he always listens. He always loves us. And he always helps us through our times of trouble, so let's ask for his help.

Ask kids to form pairs and discuss with their partner how they need God's protection in their lives now. Give kids several minutes to talk and then ask them to silently pray for each other, letting them know you'll close in prayer.

Allow time.

PRAY:

Dear God, thank you for your protection. Thank you for your love. And thank you for hearing us. We know you work all things for our good as we love and follow you. You're good to us, God—and we love you! In Jesus' name, amen.

Bible References

---

2 Corinthians 12:6-7

Explain whether God promises to always protect our health.

John 16:32-33

Explain whether God promises to protect us from having trouble.

---

2 Corinthians 12:8-10

Explain whether God always protects us from weakness.

Matthew 5:11-12

Explain whether God always protects us from bullies.

Hebrews 9:27-28

Explain whether God always protects us from dying.

Permission to photocopy this page from *13 Most Important Bible Lessons for Kids About Living for Jesus* granted for local church use. Copyright © Group Publishing, Inc., 1515 Cascade Ave., Loveland, CO 80538. group.com

Jesus' Followers Are Filled With Joy

J oy—it's that quiet, positive assurance that all will be right in the end because God is in control. It's expressed not with whoops and hollers but through confident living and a sense of purpose. It doesn't depend on situations, but on knowing God well enough to know he loves you and will walk with you no matter what happens. That's what you'll help your children discover today—and you can't do it alone. Set about leading this session with prayer and a question: Are you experiencing joy? If not, include yourself as you ask God to open up every heart to him and the joy he gives.

Scripture Foundation

JOHN 17:13
Following Jesus fills us with joy.

GALATIANS 5:22
Following Jesus produces good things.

LUKE 19:8-9
Zacchaeus joyfully gave away a fortune.

PHILIPPIANS 4:12-13
Paul was in prison but was still joyful.

JOHN 20:15-18
Mary was devastated to witness Jesus being killed on the cross, but what happened next filled her with joy.

THIS LESSON AT A GLANCE

SEQUENCE	EXPERIENCES	SUPPLIES
SET THE FOUNDATION (about 10 minutes)	***Happy Place*** Kids act out their personal "happy place" in a game and then talk about what makes a place happy.	• watch or timer
PRESENT THE BIBLE FOUNDATION (about 25 minutes)	***Why So Happy?*** Kids discover what bad things happened to three people in the Bible—and why those people weren't sad.	• at least 3 kid-friendly Bibles (preferably NLT) • 1 copy of the "Bible References" handout (at the end of this lesson) • scissors • 3 containers of play dough
BUILD ON THE FOUNDATION (about 10 minutes)	***Water Prayer*** Kids use cups of water to pray about giving God the chance to make their lives joyful.	• disposable cups of water (1 per child) • bowls that hold at least 4 cups of water (1 per 3 kids) • paper towels • pitcher of water for refilling cups

Before the Lesson

PRESENT THE BIBLE FOUNDATION: *WHY SO HAPPY?* —Cut apart the copy you made of the "Bible References" handout so each of three groups will have one strip.

BUILD ON THE FOUNDATION: *WATER PRAYER* —Fill disposable cups with water—one cup for each child. Place cups out of the way but where kids can easily reach them. Have a pitcher of water ready so you can refill each child's cup.

Happy Place

(about 10 minutes)

Welcome kids, and help them form groups of five. If you have a group of nine or fewer, do this activity as one group. Ask each group to sit in a circle, allowing space between groups.

SAY:

In your group, you'll each act out—without speaking—the location of what you consider to be the happiest place on the planet. Maybe it's your bedroom, your favorite pizza place, or even a beach on a tropical island. You decide—but you'll have one minute each to act it out while the rest of your group tries to guess the location. When time's up, you'll tell your group the location if no one guessed correctly.

Whenever a group correctly guesses a location, the entire group gets to stand up and shout "Happy Place!" Ask the first person in each group to get ready. Set the timer for one minute and say "Go!" Give a 15-second warning each time the minute is almost up, and then have the next person in the circle take a turn.

After everyone has had a turn, gather groups into one large group.

ASK:

• **What is it about the place you chose that makes you so happy?**

SAY:

It's easy to be happy if you're someplace you want to be. But what about when you can't have or do what you want?

ASK:

• **Explain whether you think it's possible to be happy when you can't have or do what you want.**

SAY:

Today we'll talk about a kind of happiness that lasts even when you're in your least-favorite place on the planet; a kind of happiness you

63

feel no matter where you are or how things are going for you.

Today we're talking about joy—let's see what God says about joy.

PRESENT THE BIBLE FOUNDATION

Why So Happy?

(about 25 minutes)

SAY:

There's something I want to test.

Ask kids to stand.

I want to test the phrase "leap for joy." For instance, "Larry was so happy when he won a free vacation that he couldn't help but leap for joy." I'd probably jump up and down, too, for a free vacation.

Here's the test: I want to see what makes you leap for joy.

One at a time, I'll call out five things that might get you leaping. If you like what I call out, give a little hop. If you love it, jump. If you absolutely love it—if it makes you super, super happy—leap as high as you can for joy. But if you don't really care, no hopping, jumping, or leaping. Just stay planted. Ready?

Pause after each of the following items to give kids time to react.

• Your school just called—they decided you're smart enough and don't have to come to school anymore.

• It's National Pet Day and you're allowed to get any pet you want— from an aardvark to a zebra.

• Uh, oh...turns out the pet you chose was a skunk.

• It's Happy Hug Day and you now need to come give me a hug.

• Larry just called and said he doesn't need a free vacation so he's giving it to you.

Have kids sit in a circle.

64

Thanks for taking my test. I love it when good things happen or I get good news. Good news always makes me happy. Here's some good news I got this past week...

Briefly tell your kids about good news you received.

Okay—your turn. Find a partner and discuss this.

ASK:

- **Describe some good news you've gotten.**
- **Explain how you felt when you got the good news.**

Allow several minutes for kids to talk. Then gather their attention and continue.

SAY:

In the same way good news makes us happy, bad news and bad things can make us sad—sometimes for a very long time. Let's meet three people who got bad news or had bad things happen—but they didn't stay sad.

Form three groups, and give each group a Bible, a "Bible References" strip, and a container of play dough. Keep a lump of play dough for yourself. Have groups give each other space as they read and discuss their assigned passage. Tell groups they'll work together to sculpt something that symbolizes how the person in their passage handled the bad thing that happened (Zacchaeus cheated people, Paul was in prison, and Mary had just watched her dear friend die). Groups can choose to build one sculpture together, a series of sculptures, or individual sculptures.

Allow about seven minutes for groups to read and work on their sculptures. As they work, sculpt a cross from the play dough you kept. Then bring kids back to a large circle. Let each group read aloud its passage, show the sculptures they created, and describe how the people in the passage handled the unfortunate situation.

After each group's turn, ask:

- **After what happened, explain why you think this person was happy.**

SAY:

Thanks for your great sculptures.

Show kids your sculpted cross.

What these people had in common was they were all friends of Jesus. No matter what was happening to them, they knew ultimately that everything would be all right because God is in control. They knew God would walk with them through the hard times.

That's why they could be so confident and happy—even when things

were very difficult. And they weren't just happy—they were joyful. They had joy in their lives because they had Jesus in their lives.

Witnessing joy is one of the ways you can tell when someone is hanging around with Jesus and filled with the Holy Spirit.

Have groups set aside their sculptures. Then have kids find a partner to discuss the following questions with. Have a willing child read aloud Galatians 5:22.

ASK:
- **How can you tell if someone is joyful?**
- **How do you think people can feel joy even during times of pain or great sadness?**
- **Explain whether your best friends would say you're joyful—or not. Why?**

SAY:

We feel joy when we know and trust God and Jesus. When Jesus was praying to God he said this about his followers:

Read aloud John 17:13.

We can be filled with joy by knowing Jesus today.

Ask children to rejoin their groups again.

SAY:

Let's do a little digging. In your small group, talk about this:

ASK:
- **Explain why you sometimes aren't joyful.**
- **Tell about a time you were sad or lonely or scared.**
- **What might've helped you feel better in that situation?**

Give groups time to talk.

SAY:

It's okay if sometimes we get scared, lonely, or sad. That happens to everyone, including the people we talked about in the Bible.

But we don't have to continue feeling that way. When we feel bad we can remember that whatever makes us sad won't last forever. But our time with Jesus in heaven is forever. No matter how bad a situation seems, we can have faith and trust that Jesus is always with us, loves and forgives us, and wants us to join him in heaven.

66

ASK:

• **What stops you from experiencing joy?**

• **What do you think would help you experience joy more often?**

Give groups time to talk.

SAY:

Let's hear what you talked about. Ask groups to share what they discussed about feeling joy more often. Continue after groups have all shared.

Let's see what we can do about what stands between us and more joy.

BUILD ON THE FOUNDATION

Water Prayer

(about 10 minutes)

SAY:

We sometimes do things that get in the way of allowing us to feel joy. Since joy comes from knowing and trusting God, things we do that hurt our friendship with God or keep us from knowing him can get in the way of joy.

Let's let go of some of those things as we pray—and invite Jesus to give us joy.

Ask children to sit on the floor in groups of three. Give each group an empty bowl, and ask kids to sit around their bowl as if they were sitting around a campfire. Then have kids each get one cup of water, take the cup back to their seat, and sit.

SAY:

We're going to pray in a fun way, a way I hope helps us all grow closer to God and feel more joy.

You'll pray with your eyes open and slowly empty your water cup into the bowl in front of you. This isn't a time to play with the water or talk.

67

Instead, picture Jesus sitting with you and hearing your thoughts.

I'll ask you to pray about something and then pour a little water from your cup into the bowl.

Pause.

PRAY:

God, we want to know you better and give more of ourselves to you. We know we do a lot of good things, but sometimes we do things that get in the way of our friendship. Sometimes we do wrong things, things you don't want us to do.

Please hear us as we silently tell you about wrong things we've done.

Pause for 15 seconds.

SAY:

If you want God's help with wrong things you've done, please pour a bit of water from your cup into the bowl.

Pause a few seconds.

PRAY:

God, we love you and think about you a lot, but sometimes we forget about you. We forget how important you are and how much you want to be important to us.

SAY:

If you sometimes forget God, please pour a bit more water into the bowl.

Pause for a few seconds.

PRAY:

God, sometimes we don't trust you. We don't believe you're watching over us. Help us trust you more, God.

SAY:

If you'd like to trust God more, please pour a bit more water into the bowl.

Pause for a few seconds.

68

PRAY:

God, sometimes we don't try to get to know you better. We don't read about you in the Bible or listen for you to speak to us. We don't talk about you or ask about you.

SAY:

If you want to get to know God better, slowly pour the rest of your water into the bowl.

Pause for a few seconds.

Please firmly hold your cup out in front of you, as if someone was going to pour something into it. And now please close your eyes as I pray for you.

PRAY:

God, please see our empty cups. Fill them with your love, God. Fill them with your grace. And fill them with the joy that can only come from knowing and trusting you.

Holding the pitcher of water, move from child to child and offer a blessing as you refill each child's cup. Use each child's name and make eye contact as you pause with each child.

If you have small-group leaders, ask them to bless each child in their small groups.

SAY:

[Child's name]: **I pray your life would be filled with God's love and grace, today and every day. May you know the joy of loving and serving God.**

Pause for a few seconds.

In Jesus' name, amen.

Bible References

LUKE 19:8-9

Zacchaeus joyfully gave away a fortune.

PHILIPPIANS 4:12-13

Paul was in prison but was still joyful.

JOHN 20:15-18

Mary was devastated to witness Jesus being killed on the cross, but what happened next filled her with joy.

Permission to photocopy this page from *13 Most Important Bible Lessons for Kids About Living for Jesus* granted for local church use. Copyright © Group Publishing, Inc., 1515 Cascade Ave., Loveland, CO 80538. group.com

LESSON 8

Jesus' Followers Are Made Holy by God's Truth

Holiness in God is hard enough to comprehend—but holiness in ourselves? How can we possibly be pure like God? Sometimes it seems like such a difficult and impossible undertaking. Yet this is what God calls us to live out in our lives. Thankfully, God didn't leave us alone to figure out how to accomplish holiness on our own—a sure recipe for failure. Instead, God gave us the Bible, our guidebook, filled with his words of truth. In this lesson, you'll help kids grow to understand the importance of filling their lives with God's holy truth—not the truth of the world.

Scripture Foundation

JOHN 17:17, 19
God's Word is truth and it makes us holy.

LEVITICUS 20:7
God wants us to set ourselves apart by being holy.

PSALM 86:11
God's ways are true and show us how to live.

THIS LESSON AT A GLANCE

SEQUENCE	EXPERIENCES	SUPPLIES
SET THE FOUNDATION (about 10 minutes)	***Getting Clean*** Kids try to clean stains off fabric.	• bucket of warm water • dish soap • ballpoint pen • old white T-shirt with ink pen stains • ink pen stain remover (available at discount and grocery stores) • large, clean towel
PRESENT THE BIBLE FOUNDATION (about 25 minutes)	***Finding the Way*** Kids help each other through an obstacle course and then see what the Bible has to tell us about God's Word and holiness.	• kid-friendly Bible (preferably NLT) • blindfold
BUILD ON THE FOUNDATION (about 10 minutes)	***Stain Removal*** Kids rewash the stained fabric to see how living in God's truth cleans us and makes us holy.	• bucket of warm water • dish soap • stained T-shirt from the "Getting Clean" activity with stain remover already applied • towel from the "Getting Clean" activity • 1 index card and 1 washable marker per child

Before the Lesson

SET THE FOUNDATION: *GETTING CLEAN* — Using a ballpoint pen, write on an old white T-shirt to stain it. (You may want to practice this experience beforehand.)

72

Getting Clean

(about 10 minutes)

Welcome kids, and tell them you're glad they came.

SAY:

I have a problem I hope you can help me with. I have this special white shirt that I got pen marks all over. It's a good shirt, and I really don't want to throw it away. Can you help me wash the pen marks out? I have soap and a bucket of warm water you can use to try to scrub it out. Who would like to help me?

Invite any kids who want to try washing it out to do so. Allow them to take turns attempting to clean the marks off the fabric.

SAY:

Wow, those are hard stains to get out! I imagine you've heard your parents or other family members say something like "Don't stain that new shirt!" Now we know why. Those stains are difficult to clean!

ASK:

- What other ways might we try to get stains out of clothes?
- Why do you think we don't want stains on our clothes?
- How is a stain on the shirt like or unlike the stains of sin we can have in life?

SAY:

I have a special stain remover pen that I'd like to try on the shirt. Let's see how it works.

Following the directions, apply stain remover to the stains and work it in well. Set the T-shirt aside on a clean towel.

SAY:

The directions say to set the T-shirt aside for a while. Let's get into the Bible while that soaks in. Today we're going to explore what it means to remove the "stains" of sin in our lives and to embrace God's holiness.

73

Finding the Way

(about 25 minutes)

SAY:

Besides those on clothes, there are other kinds of stains. The Bible says that sin is a stain on our hearts, and even though we can try to scrub it out, there's really nothing we can do on our own to remove that stain. But God wants us to be holy. How can we be holy if our hearts are stained?

Read aloud Leviticus 20:7.

ASK:

- What do you think this passage says about what it means to be holy?
- Why do you think God wants us to be holy?
- Explain why you think holiness matters—or doesn't.

SAY:

God wants our hearts to be pure and clean. God wants us to make the kinds of decisions he would make because he wants us to be like him. Making choices in life that honor God is one way to show we follow God and is a very important way to help keep our hearts pure.

We're going to play a game, and I need someone to help me.

Invite a willing child to leave the room. Have the remaining kids help you form an obstacle course the child will have to navigate. When the course is ready, have kids go into the hall and silently, gently blindfold and then usher the child back into the room. Instruct the child to find a way through the course without any help from others. Remain near the child to prevent injuries from collisions with walls or other obstacles.

After the child has attempted to find the way, let the other kids guide the blindfolded person through the obstacle course. Play a few rounds so other kids have the chance to be blindfolded and to create the course. Afterward, have kids sit in a circle.

74

ASK:

- Explain what made going through the obstacle course difficult the first time.

- Explain whether you'd rather do the obstacle course alone or have help.

SAY:

Going through that obstacle course blindfolded is a lot like trying to be holy without any help. Thankfully, God gave us help.

Read John 17:17, 19.

SAY:

God gave us his Word, the Bible, and Jesus to help us know how to be holy. And God's Word is the truth. We can trust that what the Bible says is true. Sometimes we hear things that seem like the truth, but once we investigate we find they're really not the truth. We know the Bible is the truth because it came from God.

ASK:

- Tell about something you heard once that sounded like truth but really wasn't.
- How did you know it wasn't the truth?

SAY:

You never have to wonder whether what you read in the Bible is true, because God never lies and he'll always guide us to do what's right.

I'm going to give you different situations you might find yourself in. After each one, tell me how you think God would want you to respond, and why.

- Your parents ask you to clean the bathroom. You dislike cleaning the bathroom more than any other chore. What do you do?
- You're at the store with a friend, and you don't have any money. Your friend says you should just take one piece of candy because no one will know. What do you do?
- There's a new kid at school who seems a little different. At lunch he sits by himself, and at recess no one plays with him. What do you do?
- You find a wad of money next to the road and have no idea where it came from. What do you do?
- You know a friend is plotting a mean trick on another friend. What do you do?

• You are almost certain an adult isn't telling the truth about something important, but you don't think anyone will listen if you tell or that what you say will change anything. What do you do?

Read Psalm 86:11.

ASK:
• What was easy about some of these situations? difficult?
• How were these situations like what happens in real life sometimes?
• What do you do when you don't know what choice to make?

SAY:
Sometimes we have to make difficult choices. But God gave us his Word as a guide for how to be like him. The more you know God's Word, the better you'll be able to tell what's true and make choices that please God.

Let's find out more about making good choices based on God's Word.

BUILD ON THE FOUNDATION

Stain Removal

(about 10 minutes)

SAY:
Let's see what's going on with our stained shirt.

The pen marks on the T-shirt will still be visible. Let several kids wash the fabric again with soap and warm water, and then show everyone when the stain is gone.

Give each child an index card and a washable marker. Have kids move to different places in the room and then write something that's "stained" their heart. Reassure them that no one else needs to see what they write. When they're finished, have kids come one at a time to drop their card in the bucket of water and watch as the stain is washed away.

76

After everyone has dropped a card in,

SAY:

The stained shirt and cards are just like our hearts. We make mistakes and we make the wrong choices and the stain of those sins stays on our hearts. Just like the stain remover saturated the fabric and lifted the pen marks off the fabric, when God's Word fills our hearts, it teaches us how to be holy. It helps us know how to make better choices and live the way he wants us to live. And as we saw with the cards, God washes away our sins when we ask him to. In fact, in Isaiah 1:18 God says, "Though your sins are like scarlet, I will make them as white as snow." God makes us clean and holy.

ASK:
- Describe some other good things you can saturate your heart with.
- How do these things make you holy?
- What are some ways you can get God's truth in your heart this week?

SAY:

Knowing God's truth is good, but it isn't just about that. It's also about acting on what we know about God. Tell the person next to you a specific situation you'll likely face this week at home or at school and how being holy would make a difference.

Allow time for sharing.

PRAY:

Dear God, we want to be like you, and sometimes that's hard because you're perfect and we're definitely not. Thank you for giving us your Word, the Bible, to teach us the right things to do, and thank you for loving us even though we fall short. Help us to be holy like you. In Jesus' name, amen.

Jesus' Followers Are Sent Into Mission

What does it mean to be on a mission? And what happens when you go on a mission? Some kids will know all about what going on a mission trip means, and a few may have actually gone. But what does it mean to be on a mission from Jesus—every day of our lives?

Knowing that Jesus wants us to go and tell others about him is an exciting (and even daunting) mission—one that may lead to adventures and the unknown. Use this lesson to help children know what mission Jesus has given each of us and to challenge them to consider what this might look like in their everyday lives.

Scripture Foundation

MATTHEW 28:19-20; ACTS 1:8
Jesus tells his disciples to go throughout the world and make disciples.

ACTS 4:1-21
Peter and John are arrested for teaching about Jesus.

THIS LESSON AT A GLANCE

SEQUENCE	EXPERIENCES	SUPPLIES
SET THE FOUNDATION (about 10 minutes)	***Two-Minute Missionary*** Kids send each other on "missions" around the room to encourage others or be helpful.	• timer or stopwatch
PRESENT THE BIBLE FOUNDATION (about 25 minutes)	***Missionary Me*** Kids read about the mission Jesus gave his followers and explore what happened to Peter and John when they obeyed this mission.	• kid-friendly Bible (preferably NLT) • paper or card stock • glue • scissors • craft supplies such as tissue paper, glitter glue and markers • 6 copies of the "Peter and John" script (at the end of this lesson)
BUILD ON THE FOUNDATION (about 10 minutes)	***Go Laces*** Kids make reminders of their mission and put them on their shoelaces or shoes.	• card stock or lightweight cardboard • several pairs of scissors • hole punch • pens or pencils • yarn or string

Before the Lesson

PRESENT THE BIBLE FOUNDATION: *MISSIONARY ME* — Read Acts 4:1-21 so you are able to summarize it for the kids.

BUILD ON THE FOUNDATION: *GO LACES* — You can use empty cereal boxes for the lightweight cardboard. They're colorful on one side and blank on the other, which works well for this activity.

Two-Minute Missionary

(about 10 minutes)

Welcome children, and have them form pairs. If there is an uneven number of kids, step in to be someone's partner.

SAY:
Let's play a game. The person in your pair who's wearing the most blue will be the Missionary and the other person will be the Sender.

Pause for a moment so each pair can determine who is the Missionary and who is the Sender.

SAY:
For about two minutes, the Sender will give the Missionary special "missions" to go on. These missions will all be special assignments to make life better for others in our group. For example, the Sender could say, "Go tell [name of a girl in your class] **that she has a nice smile." And then the Missionary will go do that. Or the Sender could say, "I see a piece of trash on the floor. Pick it up and put it into the trash can." And then the Missionary will do that, too.**

Set any guidelines such as whether kids can leave the room and so on. Remind kids that they can only send Missionaries on good and helpful missions. Then time kids for two minutes, having the Senders assign missions for the Missionaries to complete.

After two minutes, have everyone switch roles so the Senders are now the Missionaries. Play again with the same guidelines so everyone has the chance to be a Sender and Missionary.

After two minutes, have children sit in a circle.

ASK:
- **Explain what you liked about being a Missionary.**
- **Explain what you liked about being a Sender.**

81

SAY:

The Bible tells us that Jesus gave his followers a very important mission. Today we're going to explore what that mission is. We're also going to discover what happened to some of the first of Jesus' followers who went out on this very important mission.

PRESENT THE BIBLE FOUNDATION

Missionary Me

(about 25 minutes)

ASK:

- Tell what you know about missionaries. What do you think they do?
- If you've served someone else in some specific way, tell us what you did. (Be ready with an example of ways kids can serve others in organized and simple ways. If you've been on a mission trip, tell kids about it.)

SAY:

Most of us think of missionaries as people who move far away—as in across the world—to tell people about Jesus. These people are definitely missionaries. But here's something surprising: We're missionaries, too, even if we don't go around the world. Let's see what the Bible tells us about this.

First, here's a bit of background. Jesus died on the cross to pay for our sins—but then he defeated death. What an amazing miracle that was! And after a while it was time for Jesus to go back to heaven. Before he left, though, he talked to his disciples and gave them a mission—a very special assignment. Let's read what Jesus said in Matthew 28:19-20 and in Acts 1:8.

82

Read aloud Matthew 28:19-20. Allow a few seconds for kids to reflect, and then read aloud Acts 1:8. (Consider reading these passages a second time so kids can listen closely and consider what these words mean.)

ASK:

- **How would you describe the mission—or special assignment—that Jesus gave in your own words?**
- **What do you think these instructions mean for each of us as people who follow Jesus?**

SAY:

Jesus wants all the people who follow him to tell others about him. This applies not just to a few people and not just to people from long ago. All of us! Let's see what happened to some of the first people who took this mission seriously. Peter and John went out to tell people about Jesus, and through God's power they healed a man who'd been crippled. This made a huge scene. We can find out from the Bible what happened— but we're going to do it in a creative way today.

Have kids form six groups (one child can be a group). Briefly summarize the Bible account of what happened to Peter and John in Acts 4:1-21. Distribute the paper or card stock and copies of the "Peter and John" script, and set out the glue, scissors and craft supplies. Then assign each group one of the following roles:

- Handcuffs
- Calculator
- Gavel
- Bible
- Question Mark
- Microphone

You'll serve as the Narrator.

SAY:

In your groups, you'll have three minutes to decorate a prop that illustrates the role I just gave you. During that time, you'll also work together to read through your parts on the script. When I call time, we'll read through the script together. When it's your group's turn, one of you will stand and show the prop you made as someone else from your group reads your part.

Allow time for groups to work together. Then gather everyone's attention, and together read through the script. Afterward,

ASK:
- **Explain how you think your group's prop related to your portion of the Bible passage in the script.**
- **Why do you think Peter and John were so determined to spread the good news about Jesus?**
- **Explain why you think some people want to stop our mission of sharing Jesus with others.**
- **What are some ways we can be strong in our mission to spread the good news about Jesus?**

Invite kids to tell about times they've talked about Jesus and what happened. Reread Matthew 28:19-20 and Acts 1:8.

SAY:
The Bible tells us that God is with us. Even on a challenging mission, God's with us all the time. This can give us courage even when the mission is challenging.

BUILD ON THE FOUNDATION

Go Laces

(about 10 minutes)

SAY:
Let's make a simple reminder that can help us keep thinking of ways to "go" on this important mission Jesus gave us.

Give kids scissors and the pieces of card stock or lightweight cardboard. Let them cut out circles or squares that are a little larger than a quarter. Provide a hole punch so kids can make a hole in each shape, and set out pens or pencils.

84

SAY:

On your circle or square, write a word or short sentence that'll help you remember the mission Jesus has for you to "Go and make disciples." It might be just the word *Go!* Or you might want to write a word or draw a symbol that reminds you God is with you when you're telling others about him. Or maybe you'll want to draw a heart to show God's love or a hand to show God is with you. It's up to you.

After kids have drawn or written what they want, have them tell the group what they drew or wrote, and why.

Then show kids how they can untie their shoes and put the shape onto their shoelace, and then retie their shoes—so their reminder will be with them as they go out into the world. If kids are wearing shoes without laces, provide a length of yarn or string to tie the reminder onto their sandals or shoes. They could also tie it to a zipper, button, or other piece of their clothing.

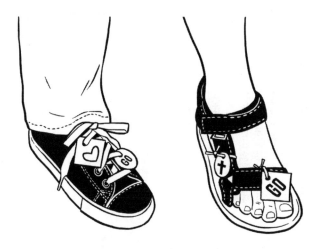

PRAY:

Dear God, please protect everyone here as we go on the important mission to spread the message of your love. Please give us courage, and let those who hear about Jesus listen and want to follow him. Thank you for letting us hear the good news about Jesus, too. In Jesus' name, amen.

85

HANDCUFFS   While Peter and John were speaking to the people, they were confronted by the priests, the captain of the Temple guard, and some of the Sadducees. These leaders were very disturbed that Peter and John were teaching the people that through Jesus there is a resurrection of the dead. They arrested them and, since it was already evening, put them in jail until morning.

CALCULATOR   But many of the people who heard their message believed it, so the number of believers now totaled about 5,000 men, not counting women and children.

GAVEL   The next day the council of all the rulers and elders and teachers of religious law met in Jerusalem. Annas the high priest was there, along with Caiaphas, John, Alexander, and other relatives of the high priest. They brought in the two disciples and demanded, "By what power, or in whose name, have you done this?"

BIBLE   Then Peter, filled with the Holy Spirit, said to them, "Rulers and elders of our people, are we being questioned today because we've done a good deed for a crippled man? Do you want to know how he was healed? Let me clearly state to all of you and to all the people of Israel that he was healed by the powerful name of Jesus Christ the Nazarene, the man you crucified but whom God raised from the dead. For Jesus is the one referred to in the Scriptures, where it says, 'The stone that you builders rejected has now become the cornerstone.' There is salvation in no one else! God has given no other name under heaven by which we must be saved."

NARRATOR   Peter is obeying the important mission of telling others about Jesus. Pretty exciting—but also scary, too, since he was in front of the court. Let's see what happened next.

GAVEL   The members of the council were amazed when they saw the boldness of Peter and John, for they could see that they were ordinary men with no special training in the Scriptures. They also recognized them as men who had been with Jesus. But since they could see the man who had been healed standing right there among them, there was nothing the council could say. So they ordered Peter and John out of the council chamber and conferred among themselves.

QUESTION MARK   "What should we do with these men?" they asked each other. "We can't deny that they have performed a miraculous sign, and everybody in Jerusalem knows about it. But to keep them from spreading their propaganda any further, we must warn them not to speak to anyone in Jesus' name again." So they called the apostles back in and commanded them never again to speak or teach in the name of Jesus.

MICROPHONE   But Peter and John replied, "Do you think God wants us to obey you rather than him? We cannot stop telling about everything we have seen and heard."

HANDCUFFS   The council then threatened them further, but they finally let them go because they didn't know how to punish them without starting a riot.

NARRATOR   Peter and John went on a mission to tell others about Jesus—and the good news is thousands of people listened and began to follow Jesus. What must've been scary is that there were people who didn't want to hear about Jesus. These people had the power to make life very difficult for people who followed Jesus.

There are still parts of the world where anyone who talks about Jesus is put into jail, hurt, and even put to death. Even at school or other places you might go there are people who don't want us to talk about Jesus.

Permission to photocopy this page from *13 Most Important Bible Lessons for Kids About Living for Jesus* granted for local church use.
Copyright © Group Publishing, Inc., 1515 Cascade Ave., Loveland, CO 80538. group.com

LESSON 10

Jesus' Followers Share Their Faith With Others

Kids today are growing up in a culture that's increasingly unChristian. While popular media appears accepting and tolerant of nearly any belief system, it often seems as though Christianity isn't as welcome in our diverse society. For that reason, kids can struggle with the courage to share their faith in Jesus. Kids may be afraid they'll be teased, rejected, or asked questions they don't know how to answer. Yet Jesus' first followers faced even more persecution and oppression than most of us can even imagine. And without their boldness, Jesus' message would've died thousands of years ago. Use this lesson for kids to discover the world-changing task Jesus has given them, and strengthen them to boldly tell people of their love and faith in Jesus.

Scripture Foundation

JOHN 17:20
Jesus prays for the people who'll come to know him through his followers.

MATTHEW 28:19-20
Jesus tells his followers to share the news of God's love and forgiveness.

ACTS 16:16-34
Paul and Silas share about Jesus, even while in prison.

PSALM 71:15
David proclaims God's power and righteousness.

THIS LESSON AT A GLANCE

SEQUENCE	EXPERIENCES	SUPPLIES
SET THE FOUNDATION (about 10 minutes)	**Save Me!** Kids play Freeze Tag two ways and talk about the important job Jesus gave us.	• kid-friendly Bible (preferably NLT) • bag of treats
PRESENT THE BIBLE FOUNDATION (about 25 minutes)	**Sticky Faith** Kids explore the Bible passage of Paul and Silas in prison and see how Jesus' followers faithfully told everyone about him.	• kid-friendly Bible (preferably NLT) • red dot (or heart) stickers (4 per child) • scissors • pens
BUILD ON THE FOUNDATION (about 10 minutes)	**Break Out** Kids examine fears that "chain" us and keep us from sharing our faith in Jesus, and then celebrate our power in Jesus.	• kid-friendly Bible (preferably NLT) • 1x4-inch strips of paper (5 per child) • tape • markers

Before the Lesson

SET THE FOUNDATION: SAVE ME!—Determine game area boundaries, keeping the area relatively small and clear of obstacles so kids are quickly tagged.

PRESENT THE BIBLE FOUNDATION: STICKY FAITH—Cut sheets of red dot stickers into sets of three. You'll need one set of three stickers for each child to take home, plus one additional sticker per child. You can find red dot stickers at most office supply or discount stores. For extra impact, draw a heart (or have kids draw a heart) on each sticker or purchase heart-shaped stickers.

SET THE FOUNDATION

Save Me!

(about 10 minutes)

Welcome kids, and explain that they're going to play a game. Point out the game area boundaries you determined beforehand. (The goal is to have most kids tagged, so keep the game area fairly small.) Choose one child to be "It."

SAY:

When I say "go," It will try to tag you. If you get tagged, sit where you are. You're stuck there! But if *I* come along and tap you on the head, you're unstuck and can get up and play again. Anyone standing at the end of the game gets a treat. Hold up the bag of treats. **Ready? Go!**

Play the game for about 30 seconds, quickly tagging all seated kids so they can continue to play. After 30 seconds, have kids stop where they are. Give kids who are standing a treat but don't let them eat it yet. Then leave the game area with dramatic weariness.

SAY:

This game is really fun, but I'm tired. And I thought I heard someone tease me because I'm not a fast runner. I don't want to get teased again, so I'm sitting out. You guys keep playing. Ready? Go!

Kids may ask whether one of them can take over your role, but don't let anyone be the "untagger."

Let kids continue playing until nearly everyone's sitting down.

SAY:

Wow, not very many of you are still standing. That means not very many of you qualify for a treat. Have all the kids sit.

ASK:
- **Explain whether you think my role in this game was important.**
- **Describe what happened when I left the game.**
- **Explain what you were thinking when only a few people qualified for a treat.**

89

Hand out treats so that every child gets at least one, and let them enjoy their treats.

SAY:

I had an important job in the game. When I played, there was a good chance that everyone would get a treat. When I was out of the game, almost no one got the treat. This reminds me of an important job Jesus gave us. The job is very clear and it's written right in the Bible.

Read aloud Matthew 28:19-20.

ASK:

- **How does the job in this passage remind you of my job in the game?**
- **Explain why you think people often don't do the job Jesus gave them.**

SAY:

Jesus' followers are called to share their faith in Jesus with others, because when we do, other people get the chance to have a friendship with Jesus, too. And when we all share our faith, then the word about Jesus spreads to many, many other people. That's better than any treat I could bring, but our game was a great example of how one person can make a good impact on many others if we choose to participate in the assignment Jesus gave us.

Have kids finish their treats and clean up before you begin the next activity.

PRESENT THE BIBLE FOUNDATION

Sticky Faith

(about 25 minutes)

SAY:

We discussed how people don't tell about Jesus because (name some of the answers kids gave in the previous activity). **Those are good points and true**

today—but people also felt the same way back in Bible times. For people at that time, it was very dangerous to be one of Jesus' followers—maybe even life-threatening.

People died because they talked about Jesus. Even so, that didn't stop Jesus' brave and dedicated friends from doing the job Jesus had given them. Let's look at two guys who really went out of their way to share their faith in Jesus. Hold up a red sticker. You'll see that they left the mark of Jesus' love on a lot of people.

Ask for two willing kids to be Paul and Silas. Hand Paul and Silas each several sheets of stickers.

SAY:
Paul and Silas loved God and had devoted their lives to telling people about Jesus. One day, they met a slave girl who had a bad spirit inside her. (Invite a girl to stand with Paul and Silas.) With Jesus' power, Paul and Silas told the spirit to leave her—and it did!

Have either Paul or Silas put a sticker on the girl, and ask her to remain standing.
This girl's life was changed!
The slave girl's owners didn't like that, so they had Paul and Silas beaten twice and then put in stocks, which are really uncomfortable wooden blocks that prevent you from moving your legs. Then soldiers threw Paul and Silas in jail. We're going to pause here for a second. Find two friends and make a small circle. We'll all discuss this question; Paul and Silas, you can talk with our slave girl about this question.

ASK:
• Tell about a time you were hurt, made to feel bad, or got in trouble for telling others about your faith in Jesus.

Allow groups a few minutes to talk, and then ask a few groups to report what they talked about.

SAY:
Well, Paul and Silas didn't let beatings, prison, or stocks stop them from sharing their faith in Jesus. In prison, they started praying and singing about Jesus.

Lead Paul, Silas, and the girl in singing "Jesus Loves Me."

SAY:

The entire prison heard them pray. All the prisoners and guards heard them sing praises to God. Have Paul and Silas put stickers on half of the kids in the room, and have those kids stand.

But then something crazy happened. There was an earthquake that shook the prison so hard that the prisoners' chains popped off and the doors flew open.

Have kids stomp their feet to make an "earthquake."

SAY:

The jailer (invite a child from the "unstickered" kids) **ran in and when he saw that the doors were open, he pulled out his sword and was going to kill himself. He knew he'd be in huge trouble if all the prisoners escaped while he was in charge. But Paul and Silas told him to stop. The jailer was so thankful that he fell at Paul and Silas' feet and asked, "What must I do to be saved?" Paul and Silas got to tell him about Jesus** (have Paul or Silas put a sticker on the jailer and let this child remain standing) **and they told his entire household about Jesus. That meant the jailer's wife, kids, and servants.**

Let Paul and Silas put stickers on the rest of the kids, and have them all stand.

ASK:

- **Look around the room. Explain what happened when Paul and Silas—just two guys—shared their faith in Jesus.**

Have everyone sit.

ASK:

- **Describe some things that could've stopped Paul and Silas from telling others about Jesus.**
- **Why do you think Paul and Silas set aside their fears and told others about Jesus?**

Distribute pens, and hand each child three stickers, being sure to keep the stickers on their backing. Ask kids to think of the names of up to three people who don't know Jesus, and have kids write the first name of one person on each sticker.

92

SAY:

All kinds of things can keep you from telling those people about your faith in Jesus. But God is bigger than your fears, worries, or questions. God loves each of those people just as much as he loves you. God loved each of them enough to let Jesus die for them—just as Jesus died for you. Listen to what Jesus prayed just before he was arrested and taken to the cross.

Read aloud John 17:20.

Jesus prayed for the people who don't yet know him and who you can share your faith with. He prayed for them and you before you were even born. He prayed for them before any of us became Jesus' followers. Jesus loves people, and that's why he wants his followers to share their faith in him.

Encourage kids to take home their stickers as a reminder to share their faith with those people in the coming week.

BUILD ON THE FOUNDATION

Break Out

(about 10 minutes)

SAY:

There was plenty that could've kept Paul and Silas from sharing their faith. But they didn't let those things get in the way. Take a moment and think about the things that keep you from sharing your faith in Jesus.

Set out tape, markers, and the strips of paper. On each strip of paper, have kids write one reason they don't share Jesus with others. Kids might write, "I don't know what to say," "Some people believe in other religions," or "I'm afraid." Encourage kids to write on at least five strips, and let them move to different parts of the room to work if they wish.

If kids say they're bold and that they do share their faith, let them write reasons that it can be hard for others to talk about Jesus.

When kids finish, work together to make one long paper chain by making a loop out of each strip and taping the loops together. You need the chain to be large enough to wrap one time around your group, so you may need to add additional strips of paper.

After kids make the chain, gather in a tight circle. Wrap the chain around the outside of your circle.

SAY:

Jesus' followers share their faith in Jesus. That can be tough at times. Sometimes we're afraid. We don't know what to say. We aren't even sure how to start a conversation. But Jesus believes in you. When he prayed, he didn't say, "I pray for people who *might* believe." Jesus said people *would* believe. You have the power of Jesus behind you. I'm going to read a Scripture from the book of Psalms. Let's use this Psalm as our prayer. After I say "amen," step backward and let's break these chains as we commit to sharing our faith in Jesus.

Read aloud Psalm 71:15, and then close by saying "In Jesus' name, amen."

Have kids step backward and break the paper chain. Let kids take home a section of chain to remind themselves each day that Jesus gives them power to overcome their fear and hesitation.

LESSON 11

Jesus' Followers Unite With Each Other

It's not uncommon for the kids in your ministry to feel like "Lone Ranger" Christians—perhaps they're the only Christian in their family, in their class, in the neighborhood, on the team, or in a club. And as they strive to obey God and follow the Bible, kids can be overwhelmed at the enormity of facing the job alone. We all feel safer in numbers. And perhaps that's one reason that Jesus prayed for unity among his followers—so that they might strengthen each other and encourage each other to stand strong in faith. Use this lesson to demonstrate what unity looks like among God's family and how we can support each other to stand strong for God.

Scripture Foundation

JOHN 17:21, 23
Jesus prays that his followers will be united.

ACTS 4:32-37
Early Christians shared everything with each other.

ECCLESIASTES 4:9-12
A cord of three strands isn't easily broken.

THIS LESSON AT A GLANCE

SEQUENCE	EXPERIENCES	SUPPLIES
SET THE FOUNDATION (about 10 minutes)	***Untied*** Kids play with balloons that are scattered, and then with balloons that are tied together.	• uninflated balloons (3 per child) • permanent marker • 12-inch lengths of yarn or curling ribbon (3 per child) • scissors • electric fans (at least 1) • large sheet of paper • large trash bag
PRESENT THE BIBLE FOUNDATION (about 25 minutes)	***A Task for a Team*** Kids tackle a huge task alone and with a team—then share what they have to make a tasty treat as they learn about the first Christians in the Bible.	• 4 kid-friendly Bibles (preferably NLT) • cotton balls (1 per child, plus extras) • 4 slips of paper • large mixing bowl and large spoon • paper cups • 1 bag each of pretzels, chocolate chips, raisins, and ring-shaped oat cereal • 4 large resealable bags
BUILD ON THE FOUNDATION (about 10 minutes)	***Braid-y Buddies*** Kids read Ecclesiastes 4:12, and then work together to make braided bracelets.	• kid-friendly Bible (preferably NLT) • 12-inch lengths of yarn (3 per child) • scissors • reflective music and music player

Before the Lesson

PRESENT THE BIBLE FOUNDATION: *A TASK FOR A TEAM* —Use slips of paper to bookmark four kid-friendly Bibles at the following passages. Number them as shown:

1. Acts 4:32   3. Acts 4:34-35

2. Acts 4:33   4. Acts 4:36-37

Open the bags of pretzels, chocolate chips, raisins, and ring-shaped oat cereal and put each one of them into a separate resealable bag.

BUILD ON THE FOUNDATION: *BRAID-Y BUDDIES* —Make a sample bracelet.

Untied

(about 10 minutes)

Greet kids, and give each child three uninflated balloons.
Spend time helping inflate and tie off the balloons. Pass around a
permanent marker so kids can write their name on their balloons.
Then form a circle and have kids toss their balloons into the middle
of the circle.

See page 8.

SAY:

**When I say "go," you have 30 seconds to move all your balloons to
that corner over there.** (Point to a corner in your room.) **You can only touch
your balloons and you can only use your feet. Oh, and this might make it
more interesting.**

Turn on the electric fans and point them toward your playing area so they blow
the balloons around.

Ready? Go!

Begin the game, and call time after about 30 seconds. Turn off the fans, leave the
balloons where they are, and gather kids away from the balloons.

ASK:

• **Explain whether you were successful at moving your balloons to
the corner.**

• **Describe your strategy for moving the balloons.**

SAY:

Let's try again, but with a twist this time.

Give each person three 12-inch lengths of yarn or curling ribbon. Let kids find
their balloons and tie them together. Then form a circle and toss the balloon "bou-
quets" in the middle. Turn the fans back on, and then play the game again, following
the same rules. After about 30 seconds, call time, turn off the fans, and gather kids
away from the balloons again.

97

ASK:

- Explain how this round was different from the first round.
- Describe whether you were more successful the first or second time, and why.

SAY:

The first time we played, the balloons were untied. Write the word "untied" in large letters on the large sheet of paper. **The second time, the balloons were united.** Write the word "united" below "untied."

ASK:

- Describe what you notice about these two words.

SAY:

There's only a slight difference between the *words* "united" and "untied." They have the same letters, but one small switch makes a huge difference. Today we're going to explore how life is different when we live as Jesus' followers who are *united* rather than followers who are *untied* from each other.

Place the balloons in a large trash bag and move them out of the way. Kids can take them home at the end of the lesson if you choose.

PRESENT THE BIBLE FOUNDATION

A Task for a Team

(about 25 minutes)

ALLERGY ALERT

See page 8.

SAY:

When Jesus was on earth, people followed him to hear his teachings, learn about God, see his miracles, and learn what he would do next. His closest followers—called the disciples—were actually in training with

Jesus. Jesus was preparing them to lead and teach and do miracles after he returned to heaven.

That was a huge job! There were only a handful of disciples but an entire planet that didn't know about Jesus. Let's see what a huge, difficult task they had.

Gather kids at one end of the room, and have them sit. Give each child a cotton ball. Explain that the cotton ball represents the message of God's love—the message that Jesus had come to earth to show and share.

SAY:
Your job is to get the message—your cotton ball—to touch each wall of this room one time and then bring it back to the starting place. But you can't touch the cotton ball. You can only move it by blowing on it. Ready? Go!

Give kids the chance to blow their cotton ball around the room so it touches each wall one time. If your room is particularly large, call time after a couple of minutes (or if you see kids growing weary).

Collect the cotton balls, and have kids sit again.

ASK:
- Explain what was difficult about this assignment.
- Describe how this task was like or unlike what Jesus' disciples faced.
- What do you think would've helped the disciples share Jesus' message of love and forgiveness with the world thousands of years ago?

SAY:
Jesus knew his followers had a big job to do, and he knew they'd need to depend on each other. Check out what Jesus prayed just before he was arrested.

Read aloud John 17:21, 23.

ASK:
- What does it mean to you when Jesus said, "I pray that they will all be one"?
- Explain how you think being united would help them share the message of Jesus.

99

SAY:

Let's see if being united really helps. Form groups of three, and give each group a new cotton ball. Explain that they have the same task as before—the cotton ball must touch each wall one time and can only be moved by kids blowing on it. Allow a minute for kids to strategize, and then let kids try the task again. When everyone has finished, gather the cotton balls and have kids sit.

ASK:

• **Explain how this experience was different from the first time.**
• **Tell how working with a team of people changed things.**

SAY:

Jesus' followers knew they'd need to rely on each other. Let's see what they did.

Form four groups. Hand each group a Bible you bookmarked previously and one of the bags you prepared (the bags don't need to be opened in any certain order). Set the large bowl and spoon in the center of the room. Have someone from each group read the assigned Bible passage in numerical order. After each passage is read, someone else from the group will bring the item in the group's bag to the center of the room and pour it into the bowl.

Once all four passages are read, stir the mixture and then scoop out cupfuls of the snack and give it to kids. Let them enjoy their snacks as you discuss the following.

ASK:

• **Explain what you think it was like to live in that early Christian community.**
• **Describe what you think would be different if we still lived like that today.**
• **What kinds of things keep us from being united and helping each other today?**

SAY:

When Jesus prayed for his followers to live as one, he didn't just mean his first followers. Jesus was talking about you and me and all the followers that will come long after we're gone. Let's pray and ask for God's help to live as one, working together and helping other Christians around us.

Have kids form a circle and link arms.

PRAY:

Dear God, we're thankful for the chance to tell others about you and show others your incredible love. That's a big job. We need each other. Help us have open hearts and open hands, to live as united people to do your will. We love you. Help us love each other. In Jesus' name, amen.

BUILD ON THE FOUNDATION

Braid-y Buddies

(about 10 minutes)

SAY:

In Bible times, to tell others that you followed Jesus was risky. Remember, Jesus had died a *criminal's* death. Not everyone liked or believed in him. People might've thought you were weird, crazy, or even disobeying God if you proclaimed belief in Jesus. People laughed at the first Christians. People hurt them.

ASK:

- Explain whether you think that's like or unlike how it is to follow Jesus today.
- What would help you stand up for God when you feel alone?

SAY:

There's another passage in the Bible that gives us a great tool for facing hard times.

Read aloud Ecclesiastes 4:9-12.

SAY:

Think of two people you know who are Christians and need help standing up for God. It may be someone at school. It may be someone in your family or someone at church. You don't have to say the names out loud.

101

While kids think, give each child three 12-inch lengths of yarn.

Each strand of yarn represents a person who follows Jesus—you and the two people you thought of. To show that you're united, tie all three strands together, making one knot at the top. Leave about a 2-inch "tail."

Hold up an example of the yarn knotted together with a tail at the end. Pause while kids knot the yarn.

SAY:

In a minute, you'll work together in pairs to braid your yarn. One person will hold the 2-inch tail while the other person braids the yarn. If you don't know how to braid, partner with someone who does. Have kids form pairs.

As you silently braid the yarn, think of specific ways in the next week that you can show the other two people—the ones you just thought of— that you're united with them. Maybe you can pray for them or with them. Maybe you can tell those people that you believe in Jesus, too. Maybe you can write a verse on a slip of paper and put it in someone's lunch as an encouragement. Think of something you'll actually do. Make a plan.

Then you'll tie a knot at the end of the braid. Think of the knot as your commitment to work *with* those other Christians to help others know and see Jesus' love.

Play reflective music while kids work together. Then let partners tie the braided bracelets around each other's wrists. Tell kids that their braided bracelets can remind them to be united with other Christians. Then ask kids to join you in this closing prayer.

PRAY:

Dear God, thank you for giving us Christian friends to depend on. Help us unite with each another to stay strong when troubles come our way. Help us support each other and be good friends to one another. In Jesus' name, amen.

LESSON 12

Jesus' Followers Look Forward to Heaven

Heaven is a place most of us hope for—but actually know little about. Often we hear about streets of gold and the pearly gates, but for a kid, that doesn't mean a whole lot. But when you talk about the absence of pain, tears, sickness, and death—well, that has meaning to everyone. Almost all kids have experienced the pain of death, divorce, bullying, or other personal pain and they understand the hope of never experiencing it again. In this lesson, kids will identify aspects of heaven that give them hope and discuss why they can look forward to going there.

Scripture Foundation

JOHN 17:24

Jesus wants people who follow him to be with him in heaven.

JOHN 14:2-3

Jesus is going to prepare a place for his followers.

REVELATION 21:3-4

God will live in heaven with us, and there will be no more death, sorrow, crying, or pain in heaven.

THIS LESSON AT A GLANCE

SEQUENCE	EXPERIENCES	SUPPLIES
SET THE FOUNDATION (about 10 minutes)	***Heaven on Earth*** Kids choose the better of two options in several categories.	• none
PRESENT THE BIBLE FOUNDATION (about 25 minutes)	***Heaven Is Like...*** Kids discover what the Bible says about heaven and why we can look forward to being there.	• at least 4 kid-friendly Bibles (preferably NLT) • pictures of an amusement park, the ocean, people camping, and a hospital
BUILD ON THE FOUNDATION (about 10 minutes)	***Doorway to Heaven*** Kids create a door hanger as a reminder of what we have to look forward to in heaven.	• 1 copy per person of the "Heaven" handout (at the end of this lesson) printed on card stock • yarn or twine • several pairs of scissors • hole punch • markers, crayons, or colored pencils • reflective music and music player (optional)

Before the Lesson

PRESENT THE BIBLE FOUNDATION: *HEAVEN IS LIKE...* — Find images of an amusement park, the ocean, people camping, and a hospital. Look in magazines or print them off the Internet.

BUILD ON THE FOUNDATION: *DOORWAY TO HEAVEN* — Make an example of the "Heaven" door hanger to show kids. Pre-punch holes in the copies of the "Heaven" handout so kids can focus on decorating and writing.

Heaven on Earth

(about 10 minutes)

Welcome kids, and ask them to sit in a circle.

SAY:
Think of some of your favorite things: your favorite meal, your favorite vacation, your best friend. Think for a minute about some of the best things in your life.
Allow time.
Now I want you to tell me which is the better of two options. I'm going to name a category and two options. You have to decide which is the better option. If you like the first item, go to the left side of the room. If you like the second item, go to the right side of the room.
One at a time, list the following categories and let kids decide which option they like best. Encourage kids to have fun and interact with each other.

SAY:
Best candy: Snickers candy bar or Reese's Peanut Butter Cups?
Best summer vacation activity: swimming or fishing?
Best sleepover: grandparents' house or with your best friend?
Best soft drink: cola or root beer?
Best season: summer or winter?
Best toy: Xbox or a new bike?
Have kids rejoin you in the circle.

ASK:
• **Explain what it would be like to have a day full of all your favorite things and favorite people.**
• **You may have heard the phrase "heaven on earth." Describe what that phrase means to you.**

105

SAY:

When something is especially amazing or beautiful, you might hear someone say, "It was heaven on earth." We think of heaven as being a place that is beautiful and peaceful or where we get to do fun, exciting things all day long. But what does the Bible tell us about heaven? Today we're going to investigate what God tells us about heaven.

PRESENT THE BIBLE FOUNDATION

Heaven Is Like...

(about 25 minutes)

Have kids form four groups.

SAY:

Each group will get a Bible and a picture of a place you might go. Take a couple of minutes with your group and come up with reasons you'd want to go there.

Give each group a Bible and one of the pictures you prepared in advance. Allow several minutes for groups to brainstorm ideas, and then gather everyone's attention. Ask each group to share its picture and ideas.

SAY:

Each of those places has a purpose, something we look forward to. We go to an amusement park because it's loads of fun, laughter, and relaxation. We love the ocean because it can be warm, beautiful, and it's the best place for making sand castles. Camping lets us see the beautiful world God created and do things like hiking and catching fish. And a hospital might not sound like as much fun as the other places, but if you're sick, it's the best place to go. Let's see what the Bible tells us about why we would want to go to heaven.

Have groups read John 14:2-3 and John 17:24.

ASK:

- Explain why you think Jesus wants us to come to heaven.
- Explain whether you want to go to heaven.

SAY:

Jesus loves us so much that he wants us to be with him. Just like you want to be with your friends and the family you love, Jesus wants us to be with him forever. But he didn't tell us much about the place he's preparing for us. Most of what we know is from the book of Revelation, the last book of the Bible. Let's see what it says.

Ask a willing child to read Revelation 21:4.

ASK:

- If there won't be any death, sorrow, crying, or pain, what do you think *will* be in heaven?
- Explain how you think being in heaven would be different from being on earth.

SAY:

If any of you have asthma, guess what? You won't have it in heaven. You'll never be bullied or humiliated in heaven. If your parents have gone through a divorce and you know the pain you feel in your heart about that, you can be assured that you won't feel that pain in heaven. Heaven is all good, no bad.

Tell an age-appropriate personal experience you've had when you felt physical or emotional pain or illness or suffered the death of someone close to you, and how you look forward to no pain, sickness or death in heaven.

SAY:

Being without pain and sadness is pretty great—but heaven gets even better.

Read aloud Revelation 21:3.

ASK:

- What do you think it will be like to live with God where you can see and talk to him?
- Explain what it means to you that God will be with us in heaven.

SAY:

This is a little like what Adam and Eve experienced. They lived in a beautiful place. They didn't feel pain or suffer from sickness. They didn't know what death was, because they'd never experienced it, and they walked and talked with God every day.

Because of sin, Adam and Eve suddenly experienced all those painful things, as we all have. But because of Jesus, we can look forward to heaven and the happiness and peace that'll be there. And we can talk to God and not be separated from him any longer.

Let's do something now that'll remind us of what we have to look forward to in heaven—so much more so than even our favorite places here on earth.

BUILD ON THE FOUNDATION

Doorway to Heaven

(about 10 minutes)

ASK:
- Explain what you're most looking forward to in heaven.
- Describe what you would like a typical day in heaven to be like.

SAY:

We all look forward to heaven for different reasons. Maybe you can imagine what it'll be like to never feel like crying again. Maybe you want to ask Jesus a few important questions. Or maybe you just want to see what the streets of gold look like.

Set out the craft supplies and the copies of the "Heaven" handout. Then show kids a completed door hanger.

SAY:

We're going to make a reminder of heaven. Take time to decorate the front of this "Heaven" door hanger. On the back, write or draw the things you're looking forward to in heaven.

If you like, play quiet music while kids work. Tell kids they can cut out their door hangers and hang them on their bedroom door. Whenever they walk through their door, the door hangers will serve as a reminder that when we are Jesus' followers, one day we'll walk through the doorway to heaven. Have kids string a length of yarn or twine through the pre-punched hole at the top.

After about five minutes, gather everyone's attention.

PRAY:

Dear God, thank you for loving us so much that you sent your Son, Jesus, to reunite us with you in heaven. Thank you for making a place like heaven for us. We can only imagine what it'll be like, but we know it'll be even better than the very best things we can imagine. In Jesus' name, amen.

LESSON 12: Jesus' Followers Look Forward to Heaven

Permission to photocopy this page from *13 Most Important Bible Lessons for Kids About Living for Jesus* granted for local church use. Copyright © Group Publishing, Inc., 1515 Cascade Ave., Loveland, CO 80538. group.com

LESSON 13

Jesus' Followers Stay Close to Jesus

atch any group of kids, and it's fairly easy to tell which ones are close friends and which ones aren't. What's harder to discern may be which kids are close friends with Jesus. Because kids can't see Jesus with their eyes and hear him with their ears, they may struggle with knowing how to cultivate a friendship with him. And it's really difficult to follow the lead of someone you can't physically see or hear. So how do people who follow Jesus stay close to him? As you lead kids through this lesson, they'll discover the amazing truth that they can know Jesus, follow him, listen to him, and have a deep and meaningful relationship with him.

Scripture Foundation

JOHN 17:25-26
Jesus describes his relationship with God and with those who follow him.

JOHN 10:2-5
Followers of Jesus recognize his voice.

PSALM 23
We can be fully reliant on and trusting of God.

PSALM 145:18
Jesus will stay close to those who call him.

THIS LESSON AT A GLANCE

SEQUENCE	EXPERIENCES	SUPPLIES
SET THE FOUNDATION (about 10 minutes)	**Get Acquainted** Kids play games to get to know one another.	• an old sheet
PRESENT THE BIBLE FOUNDATION (about 25 minutes)	**Stick Close** Kids play Follow the Leader and hear Psalm 23 as they reflect on Jesus as our leader.	• several kid-friendly Bibles (preferably NLT) • slips of paper • pencils • basket
BUILD ON THE FOUNDATION (about 10 minutes)	**Closing Prayer** Kids ask Jesus for creative ideas to help them stay close to him during the week.	• kid-friendly Bible (preferably NLT) • paper • pencils • reflective music and a music player (optional)

Get Acquainted

(about 10 minutes)

Greet kids, and have everyone sit in a circle.

SAY:

Let's make sure we all know everyone's name. I'll start by saying my name. The person on my left will then say my name and his or her name. The next person will repeat this process, saying all our names. We'll continue all the way around the circle until we're back to me and I'll say everyone's name. Pay attention because this game is like studying for a test.

Play one time. Then congratulate kids and have them form two equal groups. Instruct each group to form a single-file line and have the first people in each line face one another. Invite a willing child to be your assistant.

SAY:

Now we're going to put our name knowledge to the test. My assistant and I will hold up this sheet between your teams. You'll have 15 seconds to shuffle your line so the other team won't know what order you're in. Then on the count of three, we'll drop the sheet. The first two people in line will be face to face, and the goal is to be the first person to say the other person's name correctly. It sounds easy, but you might be surprised. Then we'll raise the sheet again and your teams can quickly reshuffle. If you've been at the front of the line once, you'll stay in the back so everyone gets a turn.

Play until everyone's had a turn, and ensure your assistant switches with someone else so he or she gets to play, too.

SAY:

Let's take it up a notch. We'll play again, except this time we won't drop the sheet. You'll have to guess who's on the other side just by listening to the person's voice.

As a group, come up with a phrase everyone will say, such as "Merry Christmas!" or "Woo-hoo, I love summer!" Encourage everyone to speak in their normal voice as you play round two. Then have kids sit in a circle again.

ASK:
- Explain which round of this game you preferred—sight or sound— and why.
- How do you think this game is like or unlike what happens when we get to know a new friend?
- Describe one of your favorite ways to spend time with a new friend.

SAY:
We can practice linking names with faces as in our game, but the only way to get really good at recognizing someone's voice is to spend time listening to that person. Getting to know Jesus is like getting to know a friend. The more time you spend together, the more you'll recognize what Jesus looks and sounds like. Listen to what Jesus said to God about his relationship with God and us in John 17:25-26: "O righteous Father, the world doesn't know you, but I do; and these disciples know you sent me. I have revealed you to them, and I will continue to do so. Then your love for me will be in them, and I will be in them."

ASK:
- Based on this Bible passage, what do you think Jesus says about relationships?

SAY:
The world doesn't know God, but Jesus does; Jesus reveals God to the people who follow him, kind of like the sheet dropping so you could see the person in front of you. We grow in our love for God when we stay close to Jesus and learn what God looks and sounds like.

Let's see what it means to stick close to Jesus.

114

Stick Close

(about 25 minutes)

Choose one team leader for every four or five kids. Distribute slips of paper and pencils. Have each person except the team leader write his or her name on a slip of paper, fold it, and put it in a basket.

SAY:

Each team leader will take a turn choosing a slip from the basket and then calling the name of the person that's on the slip. Listen carefully, and remember who calls your name.

Have leaders take turns choosing slips and calling out names until every name has been called.

SAY:

Team leaders, take the group of kids whose names you called on a Follow the Leader walk. (Explain any boundaries of where groups can go.) **As you walk, talk to your group so they can follow your lead and also your directions. You must cross paths at least twice with another group. You have three minutes. Ready? Go!**

Have kids find their team leader, and then allow three minutes for teams to go on the Follow the Leader walk. When time is up, have kids return and sit with their group.

ASK:

- **Explain what one word you'd use to describe this experience, and why.**
- **Describe a person you follow in real life, and tell why you follow that person.**
- **In what ways did your leader help you know where to go and what to do?**

Give each group a Bible. Have kids read John 10:2-5 and then discuss how their game of Follow the Leader was like the Bible passage. After two minutes, ask groups to share what they discussed.

115

SAY:

Jesus is our shepherd, our leader. We run to him and stick close, listening for the familiar sound of his voice. But people might wonder what Jesus' voice sounds like.

ASK:

• How do you think we can get to know Jesus' voice?

SAY:

Participating in church, reading the Bible, and praying are some important ways we get to know Jesus. We can talk to Jesus every day, and we can spend quiet time listening just for his voice. Let's read more from the Bible. We'll go for a walk together as you listen to me read Psalm 23. You'll have to stick close to me to hear the words. I'll read the passage three times. The first time, listen for one thing Jesus does for you.

Each time you finish reading, invite kids to tell what stood out to them from the Bible passage. For the second reading, ask kids to listen for what Jesus gives them. For the final reading, ask kids to listen for what the passage tells them about their relationship with Jesus.

ASK:

• According to Psalm 23, what kind of a friend do you think Jesus is?
• Why do you think it's important for people who follow Jesus to stay close to him?
• What's one thing you can do this week to stay closer to Jesus?

Closing Prayer

(about 10 minutes)

SAY:

Remember we said that participating in church, reading the Bible, and praying are important ways to get to know Jesus. We're here at church, we've spent time in the Bible, and now we'll talk to Jesus in prayer.

Ask a willing child to read aloud Psalm 145:18.

ASK:

• How would put this Bible passage into your own words?

Distribute paper and pencils to kids.

SAY:

Draw one line down the center of your paper. Then draw another line across your paper to divide it into four sections. Now think about the places and activities in your life. For example, you spend time at home, so label one box "Home." "School" would be another box, and then what do you do in the afternoons or on weekends? You've got two more boxes you could label with sports or activities. Allow time for kids to work.

The Bible promises that God is close to those who call on him. And if we're calling on God, asking him to be with us, to help us and guide us, then we're drawing close to him, too. Quietly ask Jesus to help you stay close to him in those four areas of your life, and write any ideas that come to you while you're praying. For example, maybe you can write a Bible verse on an index card and stick it in your desk each Monday to remind you that Jesus is close. Or maybe there's someone on your sports team who's difficult to get along with and you can remember to pray for patience and kindness when you see that person. You have three minutes to pray and write, and then you'll share one or two of your ideas with your group.

117

Consider playing reflective music while kids work, and then allow time for kids to discuss their ideas.

SAY:

People who follow Jesus stay close to him. And we can thank God that Jesus stays even closer to us. We can forget to be good friends with Jesus, we sin—we can even forget about Jesus—but Jesus will never leave us. Let's thank Jesus for being such a great friend to us all the time.

PRAY:

Dear God, you are such a great, big, good, and amazing God that it's incredible that you want to know us at all. Thank you for knowing us, loving us, and sticking close to us. Forgive us when we aren't good friends to your Son, Jesus. Help us to want to know and love you more. In Jesus' name, amen.

Give kids a foundation to build on!

▶ ISBN 978-0-7644-7066-0 • $19.99

13 Most Important Bible Lessons for Kids About God

Children's ministry leaders have been asking for an effective way to teach kids the foundational truths of the Christian faith. *13 Most Important Bible Lessons for Kids About God* is the answer. This practical and engaging resource will draw children closer to Jesus and help them get a firm grip on God's truths. These 13 Bible-packed lessons enable upper-elementary kids to experience, grasp, and embrace the fundamentals of their faith.

Each lesson is designed for upper-elementary kids, and includes:

- Lesson at glance
- Relational applications
- Scripture foundations
- Opener
- Closing prayer

You and your kids will get a solid understanding of what's really true about God so they can build their faith. And you, the teacher, will be fully equipped to tackle tough questions and encourage children every step of the way.

For more information:
Go to group.com or visit your favorite Christian retailer!

Kids' Travel Guide™ Series

Kids' Travel Guide to the Beatitudes

Jesus left no doubt that being a Christian can be hard; but because of God's promises, each of us can experience his blessings. These 13 Sunday school lessons help kids discover a wealth of wisdom about how to live a life full of blessings—even when things get tough. And they'll learn firsthand about all the wonderful ways God shows his love in their lives, no matter the circumstances.

ONLY $19.99 EACH!

▶ **Kids' Travel Guide to the Beatitudes**
ISBN 978-1-4707-0423-0

Each book includes 13 lessons to help take your kids on a travel adventure:

▶ **Kids' Travel Guide to the Parables**
ISBN 978-0-7644-7013-4

▶ **Kids' Travel Guide to the 23rd Psalm**
ISBN 978-0-7644-4005-2

▶ **Kids' Travel Guide to the Fruit of the Spirit**
ISBN 978-0-7644-2390-1

▶ **Kids' Travel Guide to the Lord's Prayer**
ISBN 978-0-7644-2524-0

▶ **Kids' Travel Guide to the Ten Commandments**
ISBN 978-0-7644-2224-9

▶ **Kids' Travel Guide to the Armor of God**
ISBN 978-0-7644-2695-7

All of the hands-on sessions include loads of Scripture, activities, and mementos to help kids learn for a lifetime.

Plus, you get heaps of easy teacher tips and extra creative options to make the most of your sessions. Pack your bags and buckle up for an adventure full of surprises with Jesus!

For more information:
Go to group.com or visit your favorite Christian retailer!

Group